W9-ABF-743

MODERN NOVELISTS

General Editor: Norman Page

MODERN NOVELISTS

MODERN NOVELISTS

GEORGE ORWELL

Valerie Meyers

St. Martin's Press   New York

First published in the United States of America in 1991

Printed in Hong Kong

ISBN 0–312–05567–6

Library of Congress Cataloging-in-Publication Data
Meyers, Valerie.
    George Orwell/Valerie Meyers.
        p.   cm. — (Modern novelists)
    Includes index.
    ISBN 0–312–05567–6
    1. Orwell, George, 1903–1950—Criticism and interpretation.
    I. Title.   II. Series.
    PR6029.R8Z73725   1991
    828′.91209—dc20
                                                            90–44734
                                                                CIP

Contents

General Editor's Preface

The death of the novel has often been announced, and part of the secret of its obstinate vitality must be its capacity for growth, adaptation, self-renewal and even self-transformation: like some vigorous organism in a speeded-up Darwinian ecosystem, it adapts itself quickly to a changing world. War and revolution, economic crisis and social change, radically new ideologies such as Marxism and Freudianism, have made this century unprecedented in human history in the speed and extent of change, but the novel has shown an extraordinary capacity to find new forms and techniques and to accommodate new ideas and conceptions of human nature and human experience, and even to take up new positions on the nature of fiction itself.

In the generations immediately preceding and following 1914, the novel underwent a radical redefinition of its nature and possibilities. The present series of monographs is devoted to the novelists who created the modern novel and to those who, in their turn, either continued and extended, or reacted against and rejected, the traditions established during that period of intense exploration and experiment. It includes a number of those who lived and wrote in the nineteenth century but whose innovative contribution to the art of fiction makes it impossible to ignore them in any account of the origins of the modern novel; it also includes the so-called 'modernists' and those who in the mid- and late-twentieth century have emerged as outstanding practitioners of this genre. The scope is, inevitably, international; not only, in the migratory and exile-haunted world of our century, do writers refuse to heed national frontiers – 'English' literature lays claims to Conrad the Pole, Henry James the American, and Joyce the Irishman – but geniuses such as Flaubert, Dostoevsky and Kafka have had an influence on the fiction of many nations.

Each volume in the series is intended to provide an introduction to the fiction of the writer concerned both for those approaching him or her for the first time and for those who are already familiar with some parts of the achievement in question and now wish to place it in the context of the total *oeuvre*. Although essential information relating to the writer's life and times is given, usually in an opening chapter, the approach is primarily critical and the emphasis is not upon 'background' or generalisations but upon close examination of important texts. Where an author is notably prolific, major texts have been selected for detailed attention but an attempt has also been made to convey, more summarily, a sense of the nature and quality of the author's work as a whole. Those who want to read further will find suggestions in the select bibliography included in each volume. Many novelists are, of course, not only novelists but also poets, essayists, biographers, dramatists, travel writers and so forth; many have practised shorter forms of fiction; and many have written letters or kept diaries that constitute a significant part of their literary output. A brief study cannot hope to deal with all these in detail, but where the shorter fiction and the non-fictional writings, public and private, have an important relationship to the novels, some space has been devoted to them.

NORMAN PAGE

To My Parents

Abbreviations

CE JL Collected Essays, Journalism and Letters
WP   The Road to Wigan Pier

1

Orwell's Life and Work: The Political Context

A writer who came of age in the period between the two world wars, Orwell was primarily a journalist and essayist. Upper-class by education, middle-class by background, his sense of responsibility for poverty and inequality motivated him to write. He was a compulsively autobiographical writer, interested in exploring his own emotions. His first novels, *Burmese Days* (1934), *A Clergyman's Daughter* (1935), *Keep the Aspidistra Flying* (1936), and *Coming Up for Air* (1939) all contain versions of his own life-story. Though interesting and readable, Orwell's early novels are limited by their imitative forms and autobiographical bias. Yet once he discovered ways to express political ideas in fiction, Orwell wrote two of the most powerful works of the century: the fable *Animal Farm* (1945) and the anti-utopian satire *Nineteen Eighty-Four* (1949).

As he said in his retrospective manifesto, 'Why I Write' (1941), Orwell wanted to write long, entertaining novels full of characters and descriptions in the nineteenth-century mode. But his true talents lay elsewhere. His 'power of facing unpleasant facts', interest in apparently 'useless information', powerfully synthetic mind, and gift for collecting information and making sense out of it, made him an excellent reporter. He made his living as a shrewd and prolific book-reviewer, critic, broadcaster, political journalist and pamphleteer. He wrote essays on a wide range of subjects, and three non-fiction narratives, or documentaries: *Down and Out in Paris and London* (1933), *The Road to Wigan Pier* (1937) and *Homage to Catalonia* (1938). The last is generally considered the finest.

To understand Orwell's work fully, we need to know something of the 1930s, a decade of political upheaval in England and the

1

continent. The futile carnage of the Great War of 1914–1918 and the subsequent depression had destroyed public confidence in the old ruling class and the economic system, and had weakened traditional moral and religious beliefs as well. People wanted radical changes in the social system. In Europe two dominant and opposing political philosophies, based on radically different views of man and society, challenged the old representative governments and capitalist economies. The Communists believed in social equality; the Fascists in authoritarian control.

Communists and socialists interpreted history in Marxist terms. They believed that the Great War had resulted from capitalist aggression, that the strikes in the post-war period were stages in the class struggle, that the peasants and the proletariat, or industrial working class, should seize power from the landowners and industrialists. In their view the socialist movement was international, unifying workers of all countries against the common enemy. Their goal was the classless society. In contrast, Hitler and Mussolini offered new national pride and authoritarian leadership. They were political messiahs who promised to lead their people to security and power by means of technology, industrial efficiency and military conquest. In Germany and Italy socialist movements were subverted into 'national socialist' governments, socialist only in the sense that all institutions and industries were state-controlled. The Spanish Civil War of 1936–1939, in which Orwell fought, and the Second World War which followed it were fuelled by the conflict between these two ideologies.

Like many 1930s intellectuals in England, Orwell believed political change was needed to end poverty and unemployment. He belonged to no specific party, but he believed in democratic socialism, in workers' ownership of the means of production and a state-planned economy, as the best way to diminish privilege based on birth and wealth, and create greater equality and security. Although he believed radical changes would be necessary, he did not believe that England needed a Communist revolution. He criticised contemporary socialist attitudes and policies, profoundly disagreed with British Communists over Soviet policy toward Spain and rapprochement with Germany, and recorded the progressively authoritarian nature of Soviet Communism under Stalin.

Orwell wanted social change, but was suspicious of tampering with tradition. Though passionately critical of the class system and colonial rule, he also celebrated the English character and the pleasures of ordinary life. He thought that most English people lived by sound moral instincts, by gentleness, tolerance and, in a favourite phrase, 'common decency', and that they were as immune to Marxism as they were to religious dogma.

CHILDHOOD AND EDUCATION

Born Eric Blair in India in 1903, the son of a minor colonial official, Orwell inherited an apparently secure place in the Edwardian upper middle class. But the war of 1914–1918, which overshadowed Orwell's adolescence, ruined Britain's prosperity. The slump which followed caused widespread unemployment, especially in the north and in Scotland. These were hard times for the middle classes also, especially those living on fixed incomes, like Orwell's parents when his father retired from the colonial service. Throughout the 1920s and 1930s class hostility increased as workers went on strike. Hunger marchers arriving in London were a disturbing reminder of the differences between the industrial north and the relatively prosperous south. By the time Orwell died in 1950, two wars had disrupted Britain's long stability and the largely rural England Orwell knew as a boy had become urbanised; the British Empire was in the final stages of dissolution, and Britain's international role greatly reduced. East and West had become locked in the Cold War and the Atomic Age had begun.

The first twenty-five years of his life were conventional enough. As a small child he was taken back to England by his mother, while his father finished out his term in India. The middle child between two sisters, Eric Blair had a happy early boyhood in the Thames Valley. His patriotism, a prominent theme in his books, derived from his memories of the peaceful English countryside before the war.

The young Eric was acutely conscious, however, of belonging to the rather hard-up 'lower upper middle-class'. The Blairs made financial sacrifices to educate their only son, who won scholarships, first to a preparatory school, St Cyprian's, in Eastbourne, then to Eton. Orwell once wrote that the novelist John Galsworthy 'was a bad writer, and some inner trouble, sharpening his sensitiveness, nearly made him a good one; his discontent healed itself, and he reverted to type' (*CEJL*, 1.308). Orwell's discontent, which seems to date from his prep-school days, never healed. He was one of those writers whose memories of childhood are intense and haunting, whose early experience shapes their lives, who seek to obliterate the past in adult achievements, and yet draw on these vivid early impressions in their creative work. Like Charles Dickens and D. H. Lawrence, Orwell's desire to be a writer originated in his sense of self in conflict with his environment.

In a savage retrospective essay, 'Such, Such Were the Joys', written in his forties, Orwell attacks St Cyprian's School and its proprietors, whom he calls 'Flip' and 'Sambo'. He remembers in detail the physical discomforts: the 'sour porridge clinging to the rims of pewter bowls'; 'sweaty stockings, dirty towels, faecal smells blowing along corridors' (*CEJL*, 4.347, 348); the cold, the loneliness and lack of privacy. He criticises the teaching, designed solely to cram the boys for Common Entrance and scholarship examinations to the public schools (Orwell began Latin at eight, Greek at ten), the humiliating punishments, the pressure to conform to the values of the proprietors, who professed to value intelligence and hard work but who in fact rewarded good looks, money and social status. He felt ugly, cowardly, unpopular and weak; he learned at first hand the injustice of class and snobbery. His emotions and ideals were manipulated to make him feel guilty and subservient, and he lived in constant fear of contravening arbitrary rules. The worst source of guilt was that while inwardly loathing and fearing Flip he found himself desperately trying to please her.

In 'Such, Such' Orwell interprets a small boy's experience with the sophisticated vision of an adult. The incidents and characters are embellished with many novelistic touches, notably the grimly humorous echoes of Dotheboys Hall, the grotesque boarding-school in Dickens's *Nicholas Nickleby*. It is a characteristically Orwellian piece, a brilliant polemic cast in the form of a memoir, attacking the whole educational system in which he was brought up. Some critics have urged us to read the work as fiction and sought to discount its biographical value. Though far from a 'true' account of his schooldays, the essay is a valuable description of the psychological pattern the adult Orwell detected in his childhood. Orwell drew on these insights in his novels, especially *Nineteen Eighty-Four*. Flip is a capricious dictator, and the school's customs and rituals make it a model of a totalitarian society, a closed 'world of force and fraud and secrecy', where 'against no matter what degree of bullying you had no redress' (*CEJL*, 4.349).

In an essay written in the 1930s, using more overt political imagery, the poet W. H. Auden made a similar point about his school. He attacked the 'honour system' which turned every boy into a potential informer. 'The best reason I have for opposing Fascism', he wrote, 'is that at school I lived in a Fascist state.'[1] The novelist Evelyn Waugh, at the opposite end of the political spectrum from Auden and Orwell, described the same sort of misery and conflict in his life at Lancing College: the cold, squalor and poor food, the bitterness of feeling excluded and unpopular, the morbid fear of being conspicuous and the eagerness to conform, the longing 'to remain myself and yet be accepted as one of this distasteful mob'.[2]

Orwell was happier at Eton, where he was no longer under pressure to compete. In later life he always discounted its influence and claimed to have done no work there. But he no doubt benefited from being among his intellectual equals. The novelist Anthony Powell, a near-contemporary there, has described the school's tolerance for eccentricity and its comparative comfort after the barbarity of prep school. 'Nothing could be further from the truth than the legend that no work was ever done', Powell wrote.[3] Orwell's humane and learned tutor, A. S. F. Gow, gave him freedom to choose the topics of his essays and intelligent criticism of his work. These essays, and his training in Latin and Greek grammar and translation, surely helped form his vigorous prose style.

The critic Cyril Connolly, who was at the same schools with Orwell, described his developing personality when at Eton. Connolly thought him 'schoolproof', independent-minded, indifferent to accepted values and exhortations to show school spirit. Nicknamed 'Cynicus', Orwell remained fundamentally an outsider, but learned self-preservation and acquired the mixture of 'enthusiasm with moral cowardice and social sense' necessary to flourish at a public school.[4] Connolly admired his wide reading, his daring tastes in authors such as Bernard Shaw and H. G. Wells, his professed atheism and socialism.

Because he belonged to the College, a hot-house of scholarship boys frequently despised as intellectuals by the wealthy Oppidans, or fee-paying pupils, Orwell's sense of the injustice of class privilege grew sharper. Sir Steven Runciman, an aristocratic friend, recalled that Orwell would never visit him in the holidays. Runciman was relieved when his invitations were refused. He guessed that Orwell was proud and sensitive, but says that Orwell later exaggerated his lack of money and his ugliness, and even enjoyed saying he was ugly.[5] Orwell's friend and patron Richard Rees remembered how Orwell winced, one day in 1948, when Rees used the word 'tug' (an Eton slang term for a scholar, who wore an academic gown, or 'toga').[6] Orwell's concern for social injustice originates in his own feelings of being undervalued because of his lack of wealth or status. Though he never wrote a novel about his schooldays, and never published 'Such, Such' in his lifetime, what he learned at school about snobbery, sadism and power-relationships found its way into his work.[7]

Yet his two schools taught him many valuable lessons. He had studied classics, history, literature and writing. Even the rote memorisation and examination-taking, which he scorned, served him well in his career. As a journalist he drew on his ability to produce a polished piece of work out of unpromising scraps. In spite of his cynicism about the public-school ethos Orwell had a strong sense of duty and responsibility, valued honesty and integrity, and had an almost puritanical conscience about his work. Indeed, Orwell's obsession with telling the truth, which so energised his reporting, might well have originated in the public-school emphasis on 'owning up'.

BURMA

On leaving school Orwell passed the India Office examinations for the Indian Imperial Police, opting to serve in Burma because of his mother's connections there. This seems an odd choice for an individualist, but Orwell had few prospects, had to earn his own living, and wanted a job with some independence. He had not worked hard enough to win a scholarship to Oxford or Cambridge, and it would have taken more time and money to establish him in a profession. He had probably had enough of being a scholarship boy among the 'moneyed beasts'.

In Burma, where he remained from 1922 to 1927, he worked hard in a series of provincial postings as Assistant Superintendent of Police. Well over six feet tall, nineteen years old, rather thin and gaunt, Orwell was not impressive in uniform. Aloof and intellectual, he avoided the officers' clubs, and although quite well liked he was not close to any of his colleagues. He read a great deal, was a good linguist, and took the trouble to learn about the country. His first novel, *Burmese Days*, expresses the emotional and intellectual isolation he felt. Increasingly unhappy about his role as a policeman in the Empire, when he went on leave in 1927 he decided not to return, and became steadfastly anti-imperialist. Later on he used some of his experiences in Burma to write two of his best essays, 'Shooting an Elephant' and 'A Hanging'.

EARLY WRITINGS

By now Orwell's parents had moved to Southwold on the Suffolk coast, where many of their Anglo-Indian friends had settled. From time to time he would stay with them over the next few years, but they did not understand why he had given up a secure career, nor sympathise with his efforts to write. For the first half of his life Orwell had lived mostly in institutions, which had given him an identity and caste: prep school, Eton, and the Burma Police. Now he tried to throw off that identity and make his outer life reflect his inner self more faithfully. He rented a cheap room in London where he could write and at the same time began a social experiment. Wearing second-hand clothes, he went off for brief periods to live in common lodging-houses in the East End of London. Orwell gave his reasons for doing this in *The Road to Wigan Pier* (1937). Noting that 'it is in fact very difficult to escape, culturally, from the class in which you are born', he said that he wanted to rid himself of class, to expiate the guilt he felt for his privileged life and his service in Burma. In an ironic reversal of his childish desire to be among the richest boys of the school, he declared his wish to be 'on terms of utter equality with working-class people' (*WP*, ch. 13).

But in 1927 he knew very little about the working class. At first he sought the company of down-and-outs, to relieve his guilt by 'touching bottom'. By living as a destitute man he gained direct contact with poverty and learned how institutions for the poor, such as hostels, prisons, lodging-houses and hospitals, worked; at the same time, like any tourist, he understood his own background better. He identified with the poor for emotional rather than intellectual reasons; his conversion to socialism came later. He tried to overcome his self-hatred, and saw writing about the hardships of homeless, unemployed, disabled or low-paid workers as a way of integrating his own life and work. His work enabled him to turn his worldly failure into moral and intellectual success. His London neighbour at the time, the poet Ruth Pitter, recalled the way Orwell worked at his writing. In her view he was not a naturally gifted writer, but a determined one. Certainly none of his friends or family thought he had any particular talent for writing.[8]

In 1928 he went to Paris to write and stayed for about eighteen months. He lived cheaply, working hard at stories, novels and articles, and published little. When he ran out of money he worked as a dishwasher in a hotel, a job he described in entertaining detail in his first book, *Down and Out in Paris and London*. Throughout his boyhood he had had frequent coughs and bronchitis, and he had been ill on his return from Burma. In February 1929 he fell ill with pneumonia, the first serious sign of the tuberculosis which would cause his death, and spent some weeks in the Hôpital Cochin, a charity ward. Characteristically Orwell chose to ignore this warning, and stayed in Paris rather than seek help from his parents or from an aunt who lived in the city. Much later he used his recollections of this hospital for a moving essay, 'How the Poor Die'.

On his return from Paris he lived with his parents and wrote. Frequently he went tramping and once went hop-picking in Kent. He worked for a while as tutor to a backward boy, and later tutored schoolboys in Southwold during the summer holidays. He published a few reviews and articles, and began his long association with the *Adelphi* when Richard Rees accepted his first documentary sketches, such as 'The Spike', about an overnight stay in a tramps' hostel. Throughout this period he revised the material which he shaped into *Down and Out in Paris and London*. After the book had been rejected several times (Orwell was ambitious and had sent it to Cape and Faber), his friend Mabel Fierz introduced him to a literary agent, Leonard Moore. Moore placed the book with the left-wing publisher Victor Gollancz, who brought it out in 1933.

In *Wigan Pier* Orwell said that after Burma he had considered changing his name 'to get out of the respectable world altogether' (*WP*, ch. 9). He asked Moore, 'will you please see to it that [*Down and Out*] is published pseudonymously, as I am not proud of it' (*CEJL*, 1.77–78). But when he saw the author's name as 'X' on the proof title-page Orwell decided that he had better have a specific pseudonym. Initially he wanted to hide his authorship, because he feared failure, and because he found the differences between his ordinary self and the satiric narrator of *Down and Out* awkward and embarrassing. He signed reviews and articles, even those about tramping, 'Eric Blair', a name he continued to use all his life with people who had always known him as Eric. But he found the pseudonym useful, especially when replying to readers and engaging in controversy. When a Paris hotelier complained to *The Times* about the descriptions of hotel kitchens in *Down and Out* 'George Orwell' replied. The name became associated with a distinctive style and point of view. As Orwell's reputation grew he became personally known as George.

In 1932 he began teaching at a small private day school in Middlesex, where he stayed for about a year. After teaching at another school for a few months he became ill once more with pneumonia and had to give up teaching for good. He was now working on his first novel, *Burmese Days*, which Gollancz originally rejected for fear of libel, but which was published by Harper's in New York in 1934. He then worked on *A Clergyman's Daughter*, where he used his tramping and school-teaching experiences. Since both novels were savagely critical of recognisable people, Gollancz insisted on changes before he brought them out in 1935.

Orwell moved to London in 1934, rented a room in Hampstead and worked in a bookshop. He began writing a third novel, *Keep the Aspidistra Flying*. Orwell was now launched on a literary career, but remained insecure financially. He wrote a great quantity of journalism, but chiefly for magazines with minority audiences; although he published a book a year from 1933 to 1941, until 1945 his books were published in very small printings. A heavy smoker, shabbily dressed, he wore his thick, dark hair and moustache clipped in the military manner. He usually lived on about five pounds a week in poorly heated rooms and flats, drank strong tea and ate simple food, and suffered frequent ill-health. Though of necessity he spent most of his time writing, he formed close friendships, among them Richard Rees and the poet and critic William Empson and his wife. Though shy and reserved, he liked women and had several girlfriends before he met his future wife, Eileen O'Shaughnessy, an Oxford graduate who had worked as a secretary and studied psychology. She shared Orwell's interests in literature and socialism and cared as little as he did for material comforts.

THE ROAD TO WIGAN PIER

The year of his marriage, 1936, was crucial. In January Gollancz commissioned him to investigate conditions among the miners, factory workers and unemployed in the industrial north, where he stayed for two months. His report, *The Road to Wigan Pier* (a title with an echo of Kipling's poem, 'The Road to Mandalay', and of Orwell's own Burmese past), was published early in 1937 in a trade edition, and also in a much larger Left Book Club edition. Gollancz had recently founded the club, which had about fifty thousand members in its first year, to provide a book each month for left-wing readers. The selection committee was Communist and pro-Soviet, and *Wigan Pier* was a controversial choice.

This book was a great stride forward in Orwell's development as a writer and political commentator, and contains many ideas to which he would often return in novels, essays and pamphlets. It signals Orwell's entry into the debate among socialists about ways to ease unemployment and avert the coming war. Gollancz's project offered him a perfect opportunity for his talents. It enabled him to discover a fascinating subject; to put his practical experience to literary use; to develop his techniques of argument and description and his narrative *persona*; to write autobiography and so continue in another context his exploration of self and search for an identity, an emotional ground to stand on; to write for informative and educational purposes; and, to a lesser extent, to urge action and change. It was also the beginning of his quarrel with the Left in general.

Part One, more than half of the book, diagnoses social ills, and Part Two prescribes their cure. Orwell's vivid account of industrial workers' squalid conditions shows how well he could use factual description in argument. He gives tables of weekly expenditures to show how real people try to live on poor pay, pensions or public assistance (the 'dole'); he measures bedrooms to show what 'overcrowding' really means. But it is far more than a well-organised collection of data. Orwell's eye and nose for curious details give us aesthetic pleasure, and his observations make a coherent pattern. His account of a visit down a mine, for example, is not merely a set-piece. Using the mine as a metaphor, he argues that the standard of living his middle-class readers enjoy depends on this substructure of ill-paid and dangerous work.

In *Wigan Pier* Orwell also develops his narrative voice, the 'I' who tells the story, to unify his material and further his argument. In his book reviews Orwell adopts an educated, sceptical, liberal posture. In early essays, such as 'Clink' and 'The Spike', the narrator's attitude towards the people and situations he describes, even towards his own discomfort, is detached and ironic. It amuses him when someone assumes he is a lapsed gentleman. In *Wigan Pier*, however, though the narrator is sufficiently detached to persuade us that his account is objectively true, he is also passionately involved with his human subjects and keenly aware of his own privilege in comparison with them. For example, he contrasts the way in which he is paid for his reviews, by cheque sent directly to his bank, with the way a disabled miner must take a bus and queue in the wind to collect an inadequate pension. Orwell heightens his own fastidiousness about smells and dirt to emphasise the miners' hardships: after coming up from the mine, he notes, it takes ten minutes to clean one's eyelids. He frequently mocks his own ignorance or ineptitude, thus reminding his middle-class readers of *their* ignorance.

In Part One, Orwell constructs an implicit psychological self-portrait by emphasising his role as middle-class outsider. But in Part Two the book ceases to be a report and becomes first a confession and then an attack on socialists. Aware of the subjectivity of all facts, Orwell tended to write autobiographically because he wanted to authenticate his observations and ideas by showing how they had originated in his own life. He had done this before in his preface to the French edition of *Down and Out* in 1934; he did it later in his preface to the Ukrainian edition of *Animal Farm*; in 'Why I Write' he relates his ideas about writing to his childhood and subsequent development.

Real-life episodes provide the basis for many essays, and all his novels are to some degree autobiographical.

Orwell begins Part Two by describing his own background, the strain of his guilt about his colonial service, his desire to get to know the working class and his ambition to be accepted by them. He has learned, however, that class barriers are like 'a wall of stone' or the 'plateglass pane of an aquarium'. He asserts that class loyalties and interests are stronger than political ideals. On the one hand socialists (including himself) idealise 'the proletariat' (the term made current by Marx) but do not like ordinary working men and women; middle-class socialists do not expect their radical views ever to be taken seriously. Orwell attacks what we would now call 'radical chic' – the comfortable position of feeling one believes all the right things, but need not actually exert oneself or make any personal sacrifice to right the wrong. This attitude is at best ambivalent, at worst hypocritical:

> We all rail against class-distinctions, but very few people seriously want to abolish them. . . . every revolutionary opinion draws part of its strength from a secret conviction that nothing can be changed.   (*WP*, ch. 10)

At the end of chapter 10 Orwell provocatively suggests that the Communist–socialist dream of a classless society might well be 'a bleak world in which all our ideals, our codes, our tastes – our "ideology" in fact – will have no meaning', when rule of the proletariat might mean the destruction of our civilisation. Though this statement seems part of his gadfly tactics, Orwell genuinely questioned whether the ideal of a classless society was possible, or even worth pursuing. He knew that revolution had produced untold suffering and irreparable cultural loss in the Soviet Union, where a new and more brutal ruling class was establishing itself, though it was not fashionable in left-wing circles to acknowledge that this was so.

In the next two chapters Orwell admits he is playing devil's advocate in order to show why, given the state of England described in Part One, the obvious common-sense value of socialism does not appeal to the working class. Again he blames socialists themselves: the middle-class, professional, Fabian intellectuals, who patronise the workers and enjoy thinking about revolutions; the cranks, among whom he includes vegetarians, feminists and advocates of birth-control (which he considered dangerously susceptible to state control); the doctrinaire Marxists who preach progress and the machine-age in jargon no working-man can understand. Orwell's main target is 'the intellectual, book-trained Socialist, who understands that it is necessary to throw our present civilization down the sink and is quite willing to do so' (*WP*, ch. 11). Given the choice, Orwell argues, working people understandably prefer a Fascist police-state rather than a Communist regime.

His last chapter is brief and prescriptive: socialists must enlarge their membership by uniting people on economic, not class, grounds, to include the poorly paid lower middle class; they must talk about socialism in terms of justice, liberty and decency, not Marxist slogans. This positive chapter was hardly enough to remove the sting from Orwell's attack, however. In order to forestall criticism from Communist members, Gollancz added a foreword, summarising its contents in his own terms, emphasising the merits of Part One and playing down the arguments in Part Two. Gollancz correctly perceived the conflict in Orwell between his socialist ideals and spiritual recoil from the collectivised, standardised culture he feared might result from a planned economy. But he does not give Orwell credit for acknowledging this conflict in himself; instead he simply asserts in Marxist fashion that Orwell conforms to 'the mental habits of his class' and that he has a long way to go before 'his mind can really become free'.[9]

Orwell's argument is too subjective and negative for the commissioned purpose of the book, but for Orwell the journey had another agenda, to sort out his relationship to working people. He believed that honestly confronting the differences between middle-class and working-class people was a better way to start forming a socialist party than covering up these differences in hypocritical jargon. When he criticised the patronising attitude of armchair socialists to the workers who made middle-class comforts possible, he was also criticising himself. His journey to Wigan had been spiritual as well. Although it was offensive to many Communists and their sympathisers, his provocative book was well-received and established Orwell as an independent commentator.

Orwell's paradoxical mind was capable of holding contrary views simultaneously. He often structures a piece of writing to oppose, balance and if possible reconcile opposites. He does not manage to do this in *Wigan Pier*, but he does dramatise the suffering of the poor and chronically unemployed, and confronts the difficulty of seeing poor people as human beings like oneself. The persistence of the class structure and the great number of impoverished and hopeless people in prosperous Western societies make *Wigan Pier* as timely today as it was in the 1930s.

Orwell's ambivalent desire for political change and fear of making matters worse provide the theme and creative impetus of nearly all his novels, and form the emotional background to his work. He disliked many of the social and economic changes in the south of England in the 1930s. Though Orwell disapproved of the ugly results of cheap housing, mass-produced furniture and clothing, mass transport, mass entertainment in the form of cinema and cheap paperback books, these were narrowing the gaps between the classes, and he had argued for greater political co-operation across class lines in *Wigan Pier*. A few years later, in *Coming Up for Air*, he attacked the ugly suburbs, lurid films and substandard food spawned by mass demand and mass production, made possible by increased spending power. He was never able to resolve the conflict between his love of traditional, rural England and his desire to see a new and fairer social system.

SPAIN AND *HOMAGE TO CATALONIA*

In the spring of 1936 Orwell gave up his London flat and job and rented the Stores, a primitive cottage and village shop in Wallington, Hertfordshire, which was to be his home base for the next ten years. He worked on *Wigan Pier*, gardened, kept goats and chickens, and tried to run the shop, in an effort to be self-supporting.

But in July the Spanish Civil War broke out, which was to lure Orwell away. A group of army officers headed by General Francisco Franco staged a coup to overthrow the newly elected Popular Front government of the Republic. The Popular Front was a shaky coalition of orthodox Republicans and socialist and anarcho-syndicalist labour unions, who derived support chiefly from the industrial Basque regions, Madrid and Catalonia. In the semi-feudal agricultural west and south the right-wing Church and landowning classes were dominant. The Left feared a Fascist dictatorship, the Right a red revolution. In the prolonged war which followed, the German and Italian Fascist governments aided Franco's Nationalists with men and arms, including aircraft, while the Russians supplied weapons to the Loyalists through the Communist Party. The democratic Western governments and the United States remained neutral. Volunteers from Europe and the United States went to help fight Fascism. Sympathisers saw the Spanish war as a great cause, the final defeat of the Loyalists in 1939 a tragedy, the whole struggle a dress-rehearsal for the inevitable war with Hitler.

Orwell went to Catalonia in December, intending to observe and write newspaper articles. Before leaving England he had considered joining the Communist International Brigade, but was refused travel credentials by Communist Party leaders. In this first year of the war various ill-equipped and ill-disciplined militias were formed by Spanish left-wing groups. In Barcelona, deeply impressed by the revolutionary fervour of the makeshift army, Orwell joined the militia of the POUM (Workers' Party of Marxist Unification), a Trotskyist group. They were loosely affiliated with the British Independent Labour Party (ILP), where Orwell had friends. Made a corporal in charge of a dozen men, Orwell found his Burma police experience useful. He fought in the squalid, disorganised and bitterly cold trenches of the Aragon front, about two hundred miles west of Barcelona. Sharing these hardships, Orwell found satisfaction and comradeship. In *Homage to Catalonia* he was to recall this time as his true conversion to socialism and the ideals of brotherhood and equality. Eileen arrived in February, went to work at the ILP office in Barcelona, and even visited Orwell at the front.

In late April Orwell decided that he would after all transfer to the International Brigade in Madrid, where the fighting was more intense. In May he went to Barcelona for some leave and to arrange his transfer. But a fierce struggle was developing between the dominant Communists and the anarchists and the POUM. The Communists, arguing that winning the war was the first priority, urged discipline and rule by their party; the other groups felt they should maintain their independence, and that social revolution was equally important. The Communists had the upper hand, however, because they had the Russian supplies the Loyalists desperately needed.

When he arrived in Barcelona Orwell was immediately caught up in the fierce street-fighting which erupted between the POUM and the anarchists on one side, and the Communists on the other.

He was dismayed to see former allies firing on each other and was sickened by the Communist propaganda campaign that followed. Claiming that the POUM and anarchists were in league with the Fascists in order to cause bloodshed, the Communists effectively destroyed the opposition. Many men were shot on the streets, or imprisoned and killed in jail. Orwell immediately decided against joining the Communists and returned to his unit at Huesca. Ten days later he was wounded in the throat by a sniper's bullet. By mid-June the POUM was outlawed and Orwell managed to escape with his wife across the border into France.

Gollancz, believing the Communist version of the events in Barcelona, and assuming in any case that attacking the Communists served to help the Fascists, refused to publish Orwell's book on Spain. Fredric Warburg, who was later to publish *Animal Farm* and *Nineteen Eighty-Four*, gave Orwell a contract for *Homage to Catalonia*, which he began writing in July 1937 and finished barely six months later.

In 'Why I Write' Orwell said that his chief goal had been 'to make political writing into an art' and that his creative impulse came from a sense of injustice, his need to expose a lie or inform the public of hidden facts (*CEJL*, 1.6). In his book on Spain he brought together his gifts for vivid personal narrative and for describing and dissecting a complex political situation. Although Orwell's account of the political developments is thought by historians to be inaccurate, and his knowledge limited to a brief period and a small area of Spain, it remains an enduring record of how it feels to be engaged in a military and political struggle. Herbert Matthews, the *New York Times* foreign correspondent in Spain, has said that Orwell learned little of the maze of Spanish politics, but gained 'one priceless piece of wisdom – that communism is a counter-revolutionary movement'.[10]

Spain gave Orwell important insights. When he saw police firing on workers in Barcelona he knew whose side he was on, and felt free of the burden of guilt he had borne since Burma. Fighting for the just cause of Spain also eased another burden. Orwell had been a schoolboy during the Great War, and he had been impressed by the sacrifice of many young men scarcely older than himself. Like many of his generation, he hated war and knew it to be ultimately futile, yet felt guilty that he had never fought. These street battles also showed him how Stalinist policy aided Fascists in order to attack Western democracies, when Spanish Communists followed Moscow's orders to obliterate their Trotskyist and anarchist opposition. He urgently wanted to put this message before the public.

In *Homage to Catalonia* there are two important themes: the betrayal of the decent, ordinary man by the Communists, who replace the old feudal government with one even more oppressive; and the similarities, in practice, between Fascist dictatorships and Communist regimes. Though it was Orwell's most artistically successful work of reportage, it sold few copies in his lifetime. When he put these ideas into satirical and fictional form a few years later he reached a far larger audience.

THE WAR YEARS

In 1938 Orwell was ill with tuberculosis and spent many months in a sanatorium. He was advised to go abroad for his health, and the novelist L. H. Myers anonymously gave him the money to spend the winter in Morocco, where he worked on his fourth novel. *Coming Up for Air*, published by Gollancz in 1939, a meditation on the coming war and written in the first person, was Orwell's first attempt to comment directly on the current political situation in a novel. Back home he worked on a collection of his literary and cultural essays, *Inside the Whale*, which was published in 1940. The outbreak of war in September 1939 and his long periods of illness caused him many financial problems. Medically unfit for the army, and unable to make much from wartime journalism, he spent most of his time alone in Wallington while his wife worked in a government department in London.

Orwell moved to London in 1940, and in August 1941 joined the BBC as a full-time talks assistant and later producer, broadcasting cultural and political programmes to India. At the same time he contributed to many magazines, including his 'London Letter' to the left-wing *Partisan Review* in New York.

In 1941 Secker and Warburg published his pamphlet *The Lion and the Unicorn* in a series of short books on war issues seen from a socialist point of view. This extended essay provides a useful summary of Orwell's political views. He begins by analysing the English character in contrast to the European, especially the Fascist enemy. The English, he says, are notable for gentleness, individualism and dislike of abstract thought; they value freedom and privacy, respect and believe in the principle of law. Despite their 'class-ridden society' they are deeply patriotic and act together in a crisis. At the moment, however, England is 'a family with the wrong members in control' (*CEJL*, 2.84). He believes that 'we cannot defeat Hitler while we remain economically and socially in the nineteenth century' (*CEJL*, 2.90), and that England needs a socialist revolution to unite all classes in a planned economy.

Orwell constructs a programme of radical reform to help win the war and create a better society afterwards. He urges nationalisation of industries, banks, railways; limitation of incomes, to make people more socially equal and therefore more unified; educational reform; freedom for India and the transformation of the colonies into a loose federation of socialist states. Orwell notes that the war itself was accelerating social change, as the Great War had done, and predicts that the educated middle class would be more powerful in the future. He urges the Labour Party to bring the new technologically-educated bourgeoisie to join its trade-union based membership.

He continues the attack on left-wing intellectuals begun in *Wigan Pier* and *Homage to Catalonia*, criticising their habit of comparing the English system unfavourably with Fascist and totalitarian governments. Orwell emphasises the positive value of the English way of life. Although England is not truly democratic, he argues, it is in many ways free and fair, and it is folly to pretend that the English would prefer a Fascist system to their own.

But the pamphlet also reveals Orwell's limitations as a political theorist. In his sketch of the socialist society he imagines possible in England, he neither specifies how these changes will take place, nor how they can be reconciled with the English character he has described so well. He says that the aristocracy will be abolished, but the monarchy will probably remain; educated technocrats will be in control and will crush opposition promptly and even cruelly, yet people will be free to publish what they like; the Church will be disestablished, but religion tolerated; continuity with the past will be maintained, and it will seem to outsiders that no revolution has taken place. *The Lion and the Unicorn* is as much an expression of Orwell's emotional and moral attitudes as his political views, and continues to debate the conflicting claims of revolution and conservatism, at one moment describing the need for a planned economy, at the next the 'emotional unity' of the English people.

After two years at the BBC Orwell became bored and frustrated with what he considered ineffectual propaganda and resigned in late 1943. He then became literary editor of *Tribune*, an influential socialist weekly. Throughout these years he also wrote many reviews and political articles for the *Observer*, whose editor, David Astor, became a close friend.

People who knew him well at this time have recorded his rugged appearance and character. John Morris, a colleague at the BBC thought 'his lined face suggested the grey asceticism of a medieval saint carved in stone' and commented on 'the strange expression in his eyes, a combination of benevolence and fanaticism; it was as though he saw more (as indeed he did) than the ordinary mortal, and pitied him for his lack of understanding'.[11] Anthony Powell remembered the same intent look, that 'burning desire to set the world right', in Orwell's manner and conversation.[12] Arthur Koestler, the émigré Hungarian novelist, recalled Orwell's reserve and austerity, his severity on himself and others, so that 'his enormous warmth only came out in an impersonal way in his books'.[13] David Astor noted Orwell's extreme integrity: 'One realised at once that he and his writing were the same thing, which is not at all usual with writers.'[14] Another friend, the anarchist George Woodcock, was struck by the same continuity in Orwell of the life and the work, 'the way in which his writing seemed to extend and amplify his daily conversation'.[15]

THE LAST YEARS

In the first months of his job at *Tribune* Orwell began writing *Animal Farm*, a satiric fable on the progress of the Russian revolution under Stalin, which he completed early in 1944. But the Russians had been Britain's allies since 1941, and consequently Orwell had difficulty in finding a publisher. When Warburg finally brought it out in 1945 the war was over and the Cold War (the prolonged state of hostility between Russia and her Eastern European allies and the Western democracies, culminating in the building of the Berlin Wall in 1961), when the Soviet Union became the enemy once more, was just beginning. As the Iron Curtain began to fall on Eastern Europe Orwell's book suddenly became enormously relevant: history had caught up with his imagination. A year later *Animal Farm* was published in the United States, was a Book-of-the-Month Club choice, and sold half a million copies. It made Orwell internationally known and financially secure.

In March 1945 Orwell's wife died unexpectedly. Just the year before he had persuaded her to give up her job so that they could adopt a baby, Richard. Though Eileen had been ill for some time, probably with uterine cancer, she was as stoic about her health as Orwell was about his. Reluctant to spend the money on specialist care, she did not tell him how serious her condition might be, and she died while undergoing surgery. Orwell had given up his post at *Tribune* to go as a correspondent for the *Observer* to Paris, where he had the news of her death. He returned to London briefly but went back to France and Germany, where he stayed for several weeks, and wrote about conditions in post-war Europe. He insisted on keeping his child.

From 1946 until the end of 1948 Orwell spent as much time as he could at Barnhill, a farmhouse on the remote Hebridean island of Jura. He loved its peace and beauty, but living there had many drawbacks. Food was scarce and the house lacked comforts. To reach the island from London required a two-day journey, if train and steamer connections ran smoothly. Barnhill itself lay at the end of a five-mile dirt road, far from a telephone or doctor, let alone the specialist attention Orwell needed, and as he became increasingly ill he was less and less able to enjoy country life.

Secker and Warburg brought out his *Critical Essays* in 1946, which contained pieces on the surrealist painter Dali, on Kipling, Koestler, Wells and Dickens, on comic postcards and crime thrillers, and generally discussed the relation of culture to society. The success of *Animal Farm* gained a wide audience for this collection.

Nineteen Eighty-Four, Orwell's last book, a cumulative work which summarises and develops many of the ideas in his non-fiction, was his most imaginative and original novel. Although he had been planning it since 1940, he did not start writing it until 1946 in Jura, and had finished a first draft just before he was taken ill with tuberculosis in December 1947. He spent seven months in a sanatorium near Glasgow, where he was treated with the newly developed drug streptomycin, but unfortunately he proved allergic to it. In July he returned to Jura, but his health grew worse. With great difficulty he typed the final draft of *Nineteen Eighty-Four* himself, since he could not get a typist to travel up to the island. The novel was published by Secker and Warburg in June 1949 and once again Orwell had a best-seller. The last year of Orwell's life was spent in hospitals. In October 1949, in University College Hospital in London, he married Sonia Brownell, an editorial assistant on Cyril Connolly's *Horizon* magazine, whom he had known for some time. They planned to go to Switzerland, where Orwell would enter a sanatorium, but he died in January 1950.

2
Orwell the Novelist

Many critics have observed that Orwell was not a 'real' novelist. In 1940 Q. D. Leavis praised his literary criticism and called him 'a non-literary writer who is sensitive to literature'. In her view, Orwell was wasting his energy trying to be a novelist; she praised *Wigan Pier* and *Homage to Catalonia* and said how much less convincing the latter would have been as a novel.[16] In 1954 John Wain argued that Orwell's true gift was as a 'controversial critic and pamphleteer' and that his novels 'do not add any new dimension to the ideas already put forward in the essays'.[17] George Woodcock, in a more recent appraisal, has said Orwell lacked 'the inventiveness and the power to separate characters from himself' that are necessary in a good novelist.[18] Essentially the criticism is that Orwell's novels are excessively autobiographical and ideological, that they lack the complete transformation of experience we expect from fiction.

FACT OR FICTION?

Because his excellent literary criticism, reportage and political pamphlets were poorly paid and reached a small audience, Orwell always thought of the novel as a way of making money. He admired his story-telling contemporaries, such as Compton Mackenzie, Somerset Maugham and H. G. Wells, who could entertain a wide audience, and the nineteenth-century novelists, such as Dickens and Trollope, who created varied characters and complex plots. As he confessed in 'Why I Write', he had begun by wanting to write 'enormous naturalistic novels with unhappy endings' (*CEJL*, 1.3). Even when he was working on *Coming Up for Air* in 1939 (a novel in a completely different mode) his letters mention his projected multi-volume saga (*CEJL*,

22

1.410–411). But Orwell was never to be completely successful in the traditional, realistic novel.

When he began his writing career he was in poor health, had given up a secure profession, and needed to establish a new social and ethical identity. The early novels are limited by the unresolved dilemmas of the autobiographical central character, and *Wigan Pier* is as much about 'George Orwell' as it is about conditions in the north. But his urge to inform, to reveal facts and draw conclusions from them, was just as strong as his need to explore his own personality. Orwell wanted to 'see things as they are, to find out true facts and store them up for the use of posterity' (*CEJL*, 1.4). He believed writing interpreted reality and could therefore serve a useful social function. In the essays on Dickens and on popular books and comics he appreciated the playful and fantastic aspects of literature, but he saw his own role as a purveyor of useful and sobering truths. As a novelist, then, Orwell's imagination was limited by his continuous task of self-definition and by his impulse to educate and persuade. To a certain extent the act of fictionalising, of making things up, was in conflict with Orwell's fact-finding impulse.

There are consequently two strains in Orwell's writing: the personal–novelistic and the political–polemical. His autobiographical and confessional novels reveal his personality and dramatise his experience; his essays and pamphlets inform and persuade. But these purposes overlap; his novels take up themes and use anecdotes or arguments which also appear in his non-fiction, while his essays and reportage explicitly relate every subject to his personal history. Subjective feeling pervades the critical and documentary work, and his most successful novels express political themes.

Q. D. Leavis's criticism may be valid for his first three novels, which are heavily autobiographical and derivative. But Wain and Woodcock, in spite of their admiration for Orwell, do an injustice to his original and powerful novels. Orwell used the novel for argument, adapting the realistic traditional form to the purpose of the essay or pamphlet, thus reconciling imaginative, literary aims with informational, political ones. His talent was not for dramatising particular personalities in their social relationships, but for imagining and analysing the moral and social effects of the political system. His characters tend to be one-dimensional because he saw them as representative types.

Raymond Williams has observed that none of Orwell's fictional characters are as complex or as convincing as the 'George Orwell' narrator of 'Shooting an Elephant'.[19] But Orwell did not write novels of character and manners, but novels of ideas. The more polemical they are, the more distinctive.

In his narrative essays and reportage, Orwell proposes to reveal inside knowledge, of poverty, war, punishment, the Empire. He offers to examine generally held ideas in the light of personal observation, replace vague assumptions with precise information, or lies with truth. Though the narrative may not be strictly 'true', since the material is arranged for aesthetic and rhetorical reasons, his emphasis is on the authenticity of his experience and the presentation of facts which reveal truth. Writing stories, in the sense of inventing plots and characters, did not come easily to Orwell, but the process of making sense of events which had actually happened released his creativity, and led him to emotional and intellectual insights. Orwell ultimately found ways to express these insights in the novel.

ORWELL AND THE 1930s

In his essay 'Inside the Whale' (1940), Orwell tried to define the role of the writer by analysing and contrasting the literature of the 1920s and 1930s. He cites D. H. Lawrence and T. S. Eliot as examples of the earlier period, which concerned itself with language and form, and expressed a tragic, disillusioned post-war pessimism. In contrast, the writers of the 1930s, especially W. H. Auden, Louis MacNeice, Stephen Spender and Edward Upward, valued social purpose and content over form. Writers and intellectuals who joined or sympathised with the Communist Party were excited by the idea of using their work to help form a new society. But Orwell thought that in fact they were embracing a more dangerous orthodoxy than the muddled conservatism they rejected.

Orwell's disagreement with the 'committed' writers of the 1930s was aesthetic as well as political, for he believed that no good writing could come of following a party line. In his view an artist had no obligation whatever to be interested in politics (though he could be); there was no reason to suppose that art should be socially conscious or relevant to the class struggle;

real literature can only be produced by an independent mind. 'Inside the Whale' asks whether the writer should be inside the comfortable whale's belly (like the biblical Jonah) of society, accepting its values and its rewards, or should stand outside the mainstream, and use his work to promote political change.

Orwell's whale metaphor suggests that society is stifling and enveloping as well as sustaining, and he asserts that anyone with any sense finds much to reject about modern mass culture and civilisation. But finally he defends the writer inside the whale. In this period, Orwell noted, because people felt they could do little to affect the outcome of the great political crises of the day, it was legitimate for the novel to focus on the narrow world of private lives, to keep up the human heritage of common feeling and experience. Henry Miller's *Tropic of Cancer* and James Joyce's *Ulysses* are totally unconcerned with politics, but truly expressive of how the common man thinks and behaves. Orwell believed that literature which strayed too far from ordinary life and language lost touch with its audience, and almost ceased to be literature; this was the danger with politically motivated art, such as some 1930s poetry, which was little more than propaganda. Orwell concludes that, whatever his position, the writer must observe and record his society and try to survive. The paradoxical development of this essay, which endorses the political indifference of a novelist like James Joyce, and at the same time emphasises the modern novelist's obligation to record society (an emphasis which implies a political point of view), reveals Orwell's divided allegiance: first, to the 1920s writers, Joyce, Eliot and Lawrence, who emphasise the individual's inner resources in contrast to the bleak urban context, and second, to the 1930s writers, who believed in the writer's responsibility to look outward and record his age.

The 1930s writers' sense of mission to record facts arose from several sources. Autobiographical books about the Great War, published in the 1920s and 1930s, fact-based but fictionalised for effect, suggested that real life was more interesting than fiction. Robert Graves's *Good-Bye to All That* and T. E. Lawrence's *Seven Pillars of Wisdom* are great examples of this genre. The rapid post-war social changes and the political awareness of the new generation of writers also oriented literature in the direction of factual observation of society. These writers had mostly been educated in public schools and wanted to know more about other social classes. The fashion for collecting data about ordinary life stimulated photography and documentary film-making. The Mass Observation project sent observers all over the country to record people's habits, possessions, diet, occupations. The Left Book Club was one of several publishing ventures designed to educate and inform a middle-class public about working-class life and left-wing politics.

It was a period of travel books, such as Graham Greene's *Journey Without Maps* (1936), about Liberia; Evelyn Waugh's *Ninety-Two Days* (1934), about South America, and *Waugh in Abyssinia* (1936); W. H. Auden and Louis MacNeice's *Letters from Iceland* (1937); and Auden and Christopher Isherwood's *Journey to a War* (1930) about China. These works also emphasised the author's interior journey, in which travel became an occasion to reflect on one's own values and civilisation.[20] Orwell's *Wigan Pier* is a kind of travel book, for the unemployed of the north were almost as foreign to Orwell as the Africans were to Greene, and the contrast in a way sharper. Orwell justifies including an account of his own life by treating it as so much data, assuring the reader that he is sufficiently typical of his 'sub-caste' (using the language of anthropology) for his views to be symptomatic of his class and time (*WP*, ch. 8). Orwell emphasised facts partly because it was so hard to discover the truth about tragic events in Spain, Germany and the Soviet Union in the 1930s, which Auden called 'a low, dishonest decade'. When Orwell described his gift as a capacity for facing unpleasant facts he was singling out an artistic impulse he shared with many other writers of the time.

Julian Symons, discussing the same issues as Orwell had in 'Inside the Whale', has defined the conflict in the literature of the 1930s as between the need for a subtle, private art and for public communication.[21] At the close of the decade, the defeat of the Spanish Loyalists and the betrayal of the Western Communists in the Stalin–Hitler pact destroyed the illusions of most left-wing writers. Auden and Isherwood left for New York in January 1939, giving up their political involvement. In contrast, Orwell became more politically engaged. These events made him realise that he wanted 'to push the world in a certain direction' (*CEJL*, 1.4), away from Fascism and Communism, and towards democratic socialism, that his true focus as a writer was political. With *Coming Up for Air* Orwell began to use the novel primarily to express a political point of view.

THE LITERARY INFLUENCES: DICKENS, KIPLING, LAWRENCE AND WELLS

Orwell was widely read in European literature. Of the modernists he admired James Joyce, who influenced him in specific ways: Orwell imitated aspects of *Ulysses* in *A Clergyman's Daughter*, and probably modelled Gordon Comstock in *Keep the Aspidistra Flying* on Joyce's Stephen Dedalus in *A Portrait of the Artist as a Young Man*. But Orwell began his novel-writing career as a literary realist. Reading Dickens and Kipling helped Orwell define his political position and purpose as a writer; Lawrence and Wells most influenced his form, style and themes. These writers helped shape Orwell the novelist.

Charles Dickens

Orwell's essay on Dickens (1939), an excellent piece of criticism in its own right, focuses on Dickens the moralist. It defines Dickens's social philosophy and purpose as a writer as a way of justifying Orwell's own. Orwell identifies Dickens's limitations as an artist and thinker, then argues that these apparent defects are positive qualities. Orwell notes that although he attacked public policy, such as the Poor Laws, Dickens had no organised programme for improvement; his heroes have no code of work, and desire only bourgeois security. In his novels the problems of the poor tend to be solved by benevolent capitalists, or 'Good Rich Men'. Dickens tends to be pro-capitalist, because he opposes revolution; he believes in a change of heart, not a change in the political system. He sees that society's basic problem is how to prevent power from being abused, but proposes no solution. Sceptical of revolution, he believes the new tyrant always replaces the old. Paradoxically, Dickens is a subversive writer whose works can be used to support conservative points of view (a fate in store for *Animal Farm* and *Nineteen Eighty-Four*).

Orwell argues that Dickens's view of society is moral, not political; he does not believe that political change can correct injustice, because he thinks individual men, not the social system, are responsible for evil. Dickens is a true radical because he rebels against the human condition itself; all revolutionaries are potential reactionaries, because their true aim is to redistribute power.

Above all else in art Orwell valued 'survival': the enduring appeal to a wide audience found in great writers like Shakespeare and 'good bad' poets like Kipling. Dickens's characters are grotesque, but they 'exist', and people enjoy reading about them. Dickens endures because he knew how 'to express in a comic, simplified and therefore memorable form the native decency of the common man' (*CEJL*, 1.459). These two ideas are central to Orwell as critic and novelist: that men are bound by common decency, an intuitive moral sense, independent of religion or education; and that art is valuable which can communicate serious matters on a popular level.

Orwell contrasts Dickens's moral sense to the 'smelly little orthodoxies' of current leftist politics in order to defend his own refusal to accept any party line. The business of the novelist, Orwell implies, is to describe human nature itself. The content of novels may be reduced to simple terms, because 'all art is propaganda'; a novel conveys a coded message. But not all propaganda is art. The novelist committed to promoting a political attitude risks writing propaganda, but if he denies the importance of his 'message' he may be irresponsible or irrelevant. Here Orwell touches on the same issue of 'Inside the Whale': should the writer accept the orthodox values of his culture, or should he be 'purposive', and dedicate his art to promote social change?

Orwell uses Dickens to show that, though true art may deal with politics, it cannot follow a political programme because its concerns are primarily moral. But the artist cannot be totally inside the whale either; like Dickens, the artist must always be discontented with the state of the world. The essay shows Orwell defining his political position, anticipating the movement in his novels away from private concerns to public ones, towards greater simplification (though not less sophistication), and defending his right to unpopular views. The essay is also typical of Orwell's empirical attitude: he tests theoretical positions against concrete examples, in this case using the example of Dickens's creative genius but inconsistent social philosophy to oppose the demand that writers be politically committed.

When we turn to Orwell's fiction itself we can see that he took several themes, ideas and techniques from Dickens. In the essay he refers to Dickens's childhood and discusses *David Copper-*

field and *Great Expectations*, Dickens's most autobiographical novels. The biographical parallels between himself and Dickens encouraged Orwell to interpret his past in Dickensian terms.

When Dickens was twelve years old his father was imprisoned for debt. This short period, when he worked in a blacking factory, made him dread poverty and the waste of his talents. Though it made him nervously insecure, this traumatic experience fired his immense creative energy and drive for success. Orwell read the early chapters of *David Copperfield* at the age of nine, and was deeply impressed. He believed it had been written by a child, so true was it to a child's perceptions. Clearly the novel affected the way he remembered his prep-school days; in his view he, too, had been ejected from the family into a harsh and humiliating environment, where he was threatened with disgrace and failure. But while Dickens's fear of poverty made him work compulsively to achieve material success, Orwell felt guilty about his exemption from poverty. He sought relative failure, and his novels all concern people who fail.

The theme of the child as victim in Victorian literature influenced Orwell's creation of protagonists who try to break away from a stultifying background. Orwell was familiar with George Eliot's *Mill on the Floss*, John Stuart Mill's *Autobiography* and Samuel Butler's *The Way of All Flesh*, all of which describe the struggle to form one's own moral character. Orwell extended his treatment of the child to include adults who do not mature. Isolated in a stifling and repressive atmosphere, his protagonists are inhibited and cowardly. Flory in *Burmese Days* is an outsider, stigmatised as a highbrow 'bolshie' by his ignorant companions. Like Pip in *Great Expectations*, he suffers from the desire for a snobbish and sexually cold woman. Dorothy Hare in *A Clergyman's Daughter* is a victim of her father's selfishness, but lacks the self-confidence to break out of her exhausting and pointless routine. Like Dickens's Little Dorrit, she is an immature child–woman who must bear the burden of her father's refusal to face his responsibilities.

Orwell also follows Dickens in his portrayal of schools. In *Nicholas Nickleby* and *Hard Times* Dickens attacked the schools' neglectful and abusive treatment of children, and satirised the content and method of teaching. Though 'Such, Such Were the Joys' and *A Clergyman's Daughter* were based on personal experience as pupil and teacher, Orwell's satiric targets are similar, and both works have a Dickensian flavour.

Orwell also followed Dickens in opposing working-class to middle-class values. In *David Copperfield*, for example, the improvident and impoverished Micawbers give David the unstinting love and family life which his stepfather, the Calvinistic Mr Murdstone, denies him. In *Hard Times*, the grasping Bounderbys trade their daughter, Louisa, in marriage. Like Estella in *Great Expectations*, Louisa is beautiful but cannot love. Though it is true, as Orwell notes, that Dickens properly speaking has no working-men characters, his low-class characters, when not criminal, usually stand for loving tolerance and emotional honesty, while the middle-class, when not benevolent or heroic, represent greed, hypocrisy, emotional deadness and sexual repression. Orwell's ideas about class and character are more complex than this, but this dichotomy does occur in *A Clergyman's Daughter* and in *Nineteen Eighty-Four*. Winston Smith has the Dickensian thought that 'if any hope exists, it lies in the Proles'. The opposition persisted strongly in Orwell's attitude towards Marxist intellectuals. He felt they had embraced totalitarian ideas, while no ordinary working man ever would.

Orwell noted that Dickens 'is always preaching a sermon', and Orwell also adopted a sermonising narrative voice, successfully and appropriately in *Wigan Pier*. He had difficulty, however, in managing Dickens's 'wise author' narrative method, where the narrator tells the story in the third person, is privy to all the characters' thought and conversations, and freely interjects comments. The narrator needs a confident grasp of the whole scene and story, and sympathy with the protagonist's thoughts and actions. Orwell's narrator tends to be too close to or too remote from the hero.

Dickens's characterisation is a powerful influence on Orwell's first two documentary narratives. Bozo the tramp in *Down and Out*, and Mrs Brooker, the owner of the tripe shop in *Wigan Pier*, who sits on a couch wiping her mouth with strips of newspaper, are Dickensian caricatures. The good trade-union members who steered Orwell into respectable lodgings could not understand why he chose to stay in the filthy and overcrowded room above the tripe shop. In the book Orwell omitted accounts of respectable working-class families he met, as we can see from the diary he kept of his journey. In spite of his search for first-hand experience, the literary models were a powerful presence in Orwell's writing, especially in his earlier work. Both documentaries blend observed fact and 'literary' description and characters.

Rudyard Kipling

Like Dickens and Wells, Kipling was a staple of Orwell's boyhood reading, and a writer who expressed political opinions in his fiction. There were also biographical parallels between Orwell and Kipling, who was born in India and educated largely in England, where he was separated from his parents and ill-treated as a young child. He recorded this experience in a moving story, 'Baa-Baa Black Sheep', which expresses the Orwellian theme of unjust punishment and ineradicable guilt. A war-reporter and an immensely prolific author of stories and popular verse, like Orwell he had parallel careers as journalist and writer.

In 1936 Orwell wrote a brief appreciation to mark Kipling's death. He related how as a boy he had loved Kipling, had later come to despise his imperialist views, but then had learned to appreciate his genius. In 'Rudyard Kipling' (1942), an important essay, Orwell says we should not identify Kipling with his characters, whom he observed in clubs and regimental messes. Orwell praises his vivid gallery of characters, his gift for expressing popular sentiment and for the many memorable phrases he added to the language, like 'White Man's Burden' and 'somewhere east of Suez'. (Orwell, too, was to enrich the language with new words and phrases.)

Defending Kipling from the then-current charge that his work is brutal and Fascist, Orwell points out that Kipling's belief in the rule of Law and sense of responsibility make him conservative, not Fascist. In Orwell's view, although Kipling's political judgement was distorted by his emotional commitment to the British ruling class, and his lack of sympathy for the native poor whom the British exploited, Kipling saw that Britain's prosperity came from the hard work of the less civilised and less privileged – the Anglo-Indian managers, engineers, doctors, soldiers and administrators – and he left a valuable record of their society. Orwell agrees with Kipling that, for all their faults, the men who ruled India 'did things', and changed the face of the earth for the better; he notes that if they had shared the liberal view of E. M. Forster (who believed Indians should have been allowed to rule their country in their own way) they would have achieved nothing and would not have kept their power for a week. In Burma Orwell had learned the practical necessities of policing an empire, both to maintain trade and to keep the peace between rival tribes and ethnic groups. In *Burmese Days* he tried to come to terms with the values of both Kipling and Forster.

Kipling's code of work and duty to the machine of Empire are illustrated in his stories of colonial officials and soldiers on the plains and in the hill-stations. His white heroes are self-sacrificial leaders of men, ruling for the good of the natives, who are primitive, childlike, ignorant heathen. Because the British are racially superior, their responsibilities are sacred: they have a divine right to colonise. A typical hero is John Chinn, in 'The Tomb of his Ancestors', a young man who comes out to join his grandfather's regiment in India. His grandfather had died young there, having earned the love and respect of the warlike Bhil tribe. Fearless, yet naïve and unwitting of his own power, the young Chinn establishes himself as a reincarnation of his grandfather. He kills a savage tiger which threatens the tribe, and uses his prestige to convince them all to be inoculated by the British against smallpox. Through such characters Kipling asserts the moral authority of the British to rule, the primacy of duty to the group, the value of patriotism and loyalty. Though Kipling has many other stories where men succumb to cowardice, disease or temptation, this code remains the positive idea in his fiction.

Forster's *A Passage to India* (1924) attacks Kipling's ideas. In the novel Fielding, a teacher who befriends an Indian doctor, has to face the dilemma of choosing between loyalty to his compatriots and loyalty to his friend, and he chooses his friend. Forster's Indian characters are far more complex than any in Kipling. Intelligent, sensitive, cultured and misunderstood, they illustrate Forster's charge that the British do not deserve to rule India, because they have failed to understand it.

In Kipling Orwell found stories of white men in outposts of Empire very like the place where he had spent five lonely, boring years. When he came to write his own colonial novel he tried, as Forster had, to attack Kiplingesque stereotypes. But *Burmese Days* does not resolve the conflict between loyalty to the group and to one's conscience. Orwell believed that colonial rule is immoral and destroys those who serve it, but he retained a strong sense of patriotism and duty, and was pessimistic about the colonies' future once they had gained independence. His Burmese characters are all corrupt and promise to be more exploitive leaders than the British.

Though he reacted against Kipling's political and racial views, Orwell had a certain affinity for Kipling as artist. A journalist by profession, Kipling took pains to get the facts right, in fiction and non-fiction alike. Writing about the Boer War in *Something of Myself* (1937), Kipling remarks on the number of English soldiers dead from typhoid, and connects this to the inadequacy of their latrines: 'I have seen men drinking raw Modder-river a few yards below where the mules were stalling; and the organisation and siting of latrines seemed to be considered "nigger-work".'[22] Orwell imitated Kipling's accurate war-reporting; he even has a similar paragraph on the subject of latrines in his 'Looking Back on the Spanish War' (1943). Kipling's advice on writing in *Something of Myself* may have influenced Orwell's remarks on judicious cutting in 'Politics and the English Language' (1946). Kipling wrote, 'a tale from which pieces have been raked out is like a fire that has been poked. One does not know that the operation has been performed, but everyone feels the effect.'[23]

Kipling's emphasis on fact and information appealed to Orwell's documentary tastes. One of Orwell's favourite ideas, the value of knowing or reporting something 'from the inside', actually employs one of Kipling's key phrases, which occurs prominently in 'The Enlightenments of Pagett, M. P.', a story Orwell refers to ironically in *Burmese Days*. Pagett, a naïve liberal politician, who believes that the Indian National Congress has popular support, comes out to India to see for himself. A succession of people, including Indians, visit Pagett and his host Orde, a Deputy Commissioner (whose name suggests 'order'), refute Pagett's views and strongly support Orde's imperialistic ones. The story, designed to disprove the possibility of an indigenous political movement in India, contains the sort of material Orwell would have made into an essay. Kipling's story uses 'inside' information to attack radical wishful thinking back home. Orwell adopted this technique in his political writing. He made his reputation with *Wigan Pier*, *Homage to Catalonia* and the essays, works founded on actual experience or up-to-date information which corrects popular misconceptions. This educational, informational slant, which governs his last two works of fiction, originates in Kipling.

D. H. Lawrence

D. H. Lawrence died in 1930, just as Orwell's literary career was beginning. Though Lawrence rejected England and disliked socialism, many aspects of his life and writings were similar to Orwell's. Both lived solely by writing, often on the edge of poverty; both died from tuberculosis. Typically English in their love and knowledge of the countryside, they were prophetic social critics. Both were fierce individualists who yearned to belong to an ideal community, which Lawrence hoped to found in New Mexico and which Orwell briefly glimpsed in 1937 in socialist Barcelona.

Lawrence's work dramatised themes important to Orwell: the physical and spiritual ravages of war; the decay of the English countryside and the ugliness of modern industrial towns; the hostility between social classes and between men and women; the loss of faith in traditional institutions and beliefs; and the degradation of working people who serve the machine.

Like Orwell, Lawrence thought England should change, but he saw change in individual, rather than political terms. He did not believe in equality; he was hostile to democracy because he mistrusted rule by the masses. He thought men should resist the dehumanising effects of modern civilisation, and live their lives more intensely. The most important idea in all his work is the mystical, transcendent value of sexual union. Birkin and Ursula in *Women in Love* (1920) and Connie and Mellors in *Lady Chatterley's Lover* (1928) are couples who succeed in creating true sexual harmony despite their hostile civilisation.

In 'Inside the Whale' Orwell dismissed Lawrence's idea of transcendence through sex as yet another futile 'change-of-heart' solution to social malaise. At the same time, he acknowledged that Lawrence's prediction that the future of mankind would bring either 'a wave of generosity or a wave of death' seemed unfortunately to be coming true. In fact Lawrence's sexual themes impressed Orwell so deeply that he incorporated them into most of his novels. Like Lawrence, he uses sexuality to measure and define character, and the sexual relationship to represent a microcosm of an ideal community which can challenge and subvert the social system. Inevitably, in adopting Lawrence's thematic use of sex, Orwell imitated his mode of expression; when he used Lawrentian language to describe sexual feeling he echoed attitudes which were contrary to his conscious political purpose. The undercurrent of pessimism and sadism in Orwell can be traced to the power of Lawrence's vision over Orwell's imagination.

In a review of a collection of Lawrence's short stories (*CEJL*, 4.31), Orwell recorded his vivid memory of coming across a poem by Lawrence in a literary magazine, when he was sixteen years old. It was about a woman who disliked her husband, and watches him kill a rabbit. He comes up to her and takes her roughly in his arms, his hands still bloody and smelling of fur. Orwell was struck by the connection between the killing of the rabbit and the kindling of the woman's sexual desire.[24] Insight into the sexual power of sadism, especially involving birds and animals, is a hallmark of Lawrence's fiction. In *Burmese Days*, Orwell imitates Lawrence's symbolic mode in the sensuous purple prose of the jungle scenes, which suggests Flory's entrapment and suffocation in Burma, and in the hunting episode, where Elizabeth's interest in Flory is revived when he kills birds.

In the same book review Orwell praises 'Daughters of the Vicar', a story from which he took the heroine and the setting for his own *Clergyman's Daughter*. The Lawrence story is about the struggle of an impoverished clergyman's family to maintain its respectability and superiority to the lower-class workers in the village. Lawrence contrasts the sterile middle class and Anglican Church with the vital working class when one daughter crosses class lines and marries a handsome miner. Orwell borrowed the sexual repression and impoverished respectability from Lawrence, but his heroine has no sexual awakening.

In a radio discussion about 'proletarian' literature (*CEJL*, 2.39) Orwell praises Lawrence's *Sons and Lovers* for showing working-class life 'from the inside' and injecting new subject-matter into the novel. But he generally resisted Lawrence's idea that the working-class lover, with his lack of forethought and inhibition, releases the repressed intellectual. We find this theme in the novels of Maugham, Forster and J. R. Ackerley. When Orwell idealises the working class, which he rarely does, it is from the

vantage point of a child, not a lover. In *Wigan Pier* he imagines
a well-fed father sitting with the newspaper beside a cosy fender.
His prole washerwoman in *Nineteen Eighty-Four* is an earth-
mother, not an erotic figure.

Keep the Aspidistra Flying is the most Lawrentian of all Orwell's
novels. Rosemary is reluctant to sleep with Gordon and then
does so to please him, rather as Miriam does with Paul in *Sons
and Lovers*. Like Mellors in *Lady Chatterley's Lover*, Gordon has
renounced money and society, and, like Constance Chatterley,
Rosemary is past her first youth, and becomes pregnant at the
end of the novel.

Lawrence's influence on Orwell, in both subject-matter and
style, is pervasive, sometimes overwhelming. When Orwell
imitates Lawrence's poetic and repetitive style, he produces either
the overwritten prose of *Burmese Days* or the insistent imagery
of *Keep the Aspidistra Flying*. Lawrentian echoes occur in characters' names: a Mellors crops up in *Coming Up for Air*, and Ravelston's rich, snobbish girlfriend in *Keep the Aspidistra Flying* is called
Hermione, like the dominating rich woman in *Women in Love*.
In his last novel, Orwell was able to use the Lawrentian theme
of sexual fulfillment in a new, ironic context. Winston and Julia's
love resurrects the instinctive human feelings the regime has tried
to abolish.

Though his influence on Orwell's fiction was not always
benign, Lawrence's non-fiction prose was a positive influence
on Orwell's essays, pamphlets and reportage. In his travel books
and his memoir of Maurice Magnus, Lawrence used the narrator
as both a character in the action and a controlling interpretive
point of view, a technique Orwell developed and made his own.
Orwell also imitated the concrete style, down-to-earth imagery
and colloquial argumentative tone of Lawrence's provocative
pamphlets and articles on education, religion and sex.

Orwell thought the political controversy of the age cried out
for well-written pamphlets, but they were rare. In 'Pamphlet
Literature' (1943) he praised Lawrence's 'Pornography and
Obscenity' (1929) and Wyndham Lewis's contributions to the
Enemy magazine (1927, 1929). Lawrence and Lewis were anti-
democratic thinkers who favoured authoritarian political systems
to control and organise the masses and give power to the intellectual and artistic elite. Lawrence's novel *The Plumed Serpent* (1926)
depicts the rise to power of a Mexican dictator; Lewis's *The Art*

of Being Ruled (1926) is a book-length polemic which argues that democracy is a sham, and that most men do not even want freedom. Lewis concludes that a 'modified form of fascism' in England would ensure stability and prosperity. (Lewis little dreamt, of course, how Fascism under Hitler would develop.)

Orwell praised these authors despite their unpopular views, comparing their work to the lifeless, dull and unreadable pamphlets from more orthodox sources. He valued Lewis's and Lawrence's independent wit and contentiousness, qualities he cultivated in his own work. His affinity with them goes deeper than style, however. Orwell identified with Romantic literature, which emphasises the individual in an indifferent or hostile universe, and this artistic bias clashed with Orwell's conscious commitment to socialism. The two ways of approaching experience are contradictory: the Romantic artist looks for concrete representations of his own states of mind, while the political writer, more abstractly, classifies society into groups, and identifies himself in his social role.

Though Orwell wanted to unite literary and political purposes in his work, he saw himself primarily as an imaginative writer, not a political theorist. In 1940, in a brief autobiographical description written for a reference book, Orwell names Joyce, T. S. Eliot and Lawrence as his favourite contemporary authors. All three had produced their great works in the 1920s: Joyce's *Ulysses* and T. S. Eliot's poem *The Waste Land* concentrated on the individual consciousness, as Lawrence's novels had done. Orwell consistently used these writers as a yardstick for what true literature should be. In a short piece on 'Literature and the Left' (1943), he cited these authors in a list of those attacked by the Left for being 'highbrow', and therefore out of touch with the working man; he noted that the Left were as philistine as the Right.

Indeed, Orwell used Lawrentian ideas to attack the Left's remoteness from ordinary life. In *The Lion and the Unicorn* he criticised shallow left-wing intellectuals who 'live in a world of ideas'. An important purpose of *Wigan Pier* is to show socialists that their assumptions about working-class life are false. Like Lawrence, Orwell disliked abstraction, believed in the primacy of the emotional and instinctive faculties over the intellectual and rational, and in testing ideas in the light of experience. Their somewhat similar remarks about literary criticism are revealing.

Lawrence says,

> Literary criticism can be no more than a reasoned account
> of the feeling produced upon the critic.... The touchstone is
> emotion, not reason. ... All the critical twiddle-twaddle about
> style and form ... is mere impertinence and mostly dull jar-
> gon.[25]

Orwell says,

> As a rule, an aesthetic preference is either something inexplic-
> able or it is so corrupted by non-aesthetic motives as to make
> one wonder whether the whole of literary criticism is not a
> huge network of humbug.   ('Charles Dickens', *CEJL*, 1.449)

Orwell does not go as far as Lawrence in dismissing critical
abstractions; he respected systems of ideas, but loathed the hard-
ening of ideas into dogma.

Though Lawrence was lacking in an overt 'social consciousness', he was nevertheless, as Orwell remarked, a writer with
a purpose (*CEJL*, 2.124), who claimed that the novel interpreted
life as no other form could. Lawrence believed that people should
change their relationships with one another, Orwell that the
social structure should be changed; yet Orwell was a true disciple
of Lawrence. He made the effort to live out his principles: to
put himself into a different relation to other men from that determined by his class; to fight for socialism, literally, in Spain; to
use popular art forms to relate the individual life to the political
system.

H. G. Wells

An influential novelist and social theorist, H. G. Wells was born
in the Victorian period and died after the Second World War.
His literary life and output were a formidable example, his work
a powerful influence on the form and content of Orwell's novels.
He wrote not only popular science and history, but also journalism, pamphlets, science fiction and futuristic novels. Wells sympathised with the goals of the Russian Revolution of 1917. He
agreed with the Marxist view that *laissez-faire* capitalism caused

economic insecurity and encouraged war. A public figure whose political opinions were taken seriously, he travelled to the Soviet Union, interviewed Lenin and Stalin and both Theodore and Franklin Roosevelt. Though he began his career writing science fiction and social novels, in his middle and late years he mostly wrote political pamphlets. After the Great War he worked to promote the League of Nations (a forerunner of the United Nations), which he hoped would prevent war.

A victim of poverty and snobbery himself, Wells thought the English class system out of date and wasteful of talent. He wrote novels and romantic utopias in which science in various forms revolutionises a dying civilisation. He believed, rightly, that new technology would break down the hierarchical class structure of Edwardian society. After the Grat War mechanisation brought about many social changes: new industries released people from working on the land or as domestic servants, and brought them into the town; mass-produced clothing made people of all classes look more similar; cheap bicycles and motor-cars enabled people to travel. The shortage of labour during the war opened up more jobs to women, who then demanded greater political power. In 1928 women secured the vote.

Though Wells approved of these social advances, he also explored the risks of science and technology. *The Island of Doctor Moreau* (1896) describes a chilling experiment to turn animals into men (an idea Orwell adapts for political satire in *Animal Farm*). *Tono-Bungay* (1909) is about an entrepreneur who voyages to sea to collect a mysteriously destructive natural substance, which will grant enormous power to the nation which monopolises it. These prophetic novels seem to predict medical advances in skin-grafting and the uses of radioactive minerals, and were among the first to discuss the challenges to morality brought by modern science.

Almost until his death, despite two world wars, Wells maintained that nations would use science with common sense, to bring about a better society. In his essay, 'Wells, Hitler and the World State' (1941) Orwell opposed this optimistic view of human evolution, and used the example of Hitler, who encouraged science and organised a technological society, to show that scientific advances do not necessarily go with enlightened social policy. Wells had refused to take nationalism and militarism seriously and had misjudged Hitler. In a radio talk the following year, 'The Rediscovery of Europe', Orwell, while conceding the value of Wells's pre-1914 work, dismissed him as a serious novelist, comparing him unfavourably (and rather unfairly) with Joyce and D. H. Lawrence.

Despite this criticism Orwell's essay acknowledges his debt to Wells's early novels, and grants that his ideas were the strongest intellectual force for Orwell's generation. In particular Orwell praises the series of 'lower middle-class novels' Wells completed before the Great War, the autobiographical *Love and Mr Lewisham* (1900), *Kipps* (1905) and *The History of Mr Polly* (1910), which describe Wells's personal struggle to escape from the limitations of his class and education. Wells's heroes are 'little men' who express his anger about stagnant Edwardian society. Below the rich, leisured class at the top, the majority of people led repetitive, narrow lives, with no hope of education or social mobility. Wells's novels interpreted the world Orwell grew up in, and led him to discover themes he would develop in his own work: England's decay; its bankrupt institutions, such as the Church, educational system, aristocracy and Empire; the frustrations of poverty, snobbery and sexual rejection because of class.

Reading Wells's social novels taught Orwell how to combine autobiography and criticism of the social system. In *Mr Polly*, for example, the central character focuses the narrator's anger and represents the stresses and indignities of his class. Stuck in the servile monotony of a draper's shop, Mr Polly tries to improve his lot in life, but after a series of humiliations he learns his limits. He is trapped in one restricted setting after another until he makes his final escape. Though the novel conveys Mr Polly's bitterness, the narrator distances himself (and the reader) from Mr Polly's suffering by making his humiliation comic as well as painful. Though Wells views his hero (who is, after all, a version of himself) sympathetically, the narrator remains above this little man, superior in education, more sophisticated in the ways of the world, and understands the hero's experience with the advantage of hindsight.

Orwell's plots are very like those of Wells's social novels: the protagonist rebels against an impossible situation, and tries to escape. But, while Wells effects a compromise between the characters and reality, Orwell's conclusions are often tragically bleak: Flory kills himself, Dorothy Hare returns to an empty, pointless life, George Bowling goes back to a nagging wife (and the consciousness that he can do nothing to change the inevitable 'universal smash-up'); in *Animal Farm* the animals end with a way of life no less unjust than the one they started with; in *Nineteen Eighty-Four* Winston Smith becomes completely broken. Only *Keep the Aspidistra Flying* has a truly Wellsian conclusion, when Gordon overcomes his scruples and marries.

Like Wells, Orwell defines his characters sociologically, by education, income, status, clothing, accent. Gordon Comstock's sister Julia functions in the novel as a type of frugal, impoverished spinster. Dorothy Hare's suitor, Warburton, tries to dominate her by telling her she is merely one of ten thousand shabby gentlewomen. Orwell creates type-characters, rather than particularised individuals, because he uses the novel, as Wells did, primarily to express ideas.

In his early novels Orwell had difficulty managing the relationship of the narrator to the autobiographical central character. At first he aimed at a third-person narrator who sympathises with the evolving and maturing hero, but in his first three novels the narrator ends by explaining, commenting on and passing judgement on the characters, in the Wellsian manner. In his later novels Orwell avoids this inconsistency by creating characters who are representative types: George Bowling, the average lower-middle-class man of *Coming Up for Air*; the allegorical animals of *Animal Farm*; and Winston Smith, the symbolic 'last man in Europe'.

Coming Up for Air has often been described as Wellsian because of the 'little man' hero, but Wells's influence is even more evident in the novel's narrative method. Wells often breaks up the narrative with chunks of discursive or explanatory material, so that the novel is unified not by theme, action or focus on a character, but by the narrator's argument; or he uses a first-person narrative which combines the autobiographical and discursive mode. Orwell follows the latter method in *Coming Up for Air*. There is no need for the narrator to interrupt the action or the characters' thoughts, for Bowling is the only significant character. His fluent voice conveys the meaning through description, explanation and anecdote. The narrator becomes of primary importance whenever the novel's purpose is to express an argument. In Orwell's last novel, when argument becomes even more important, the narrator seems to control the puppet-like characters in the same way that they are controlled by the party.

Like Wells, Orwell has a genius for realistic description of grotesquely dirty and degraded settings. In Wells's *In the Days of the Comet* the hero–narrator visits a friend in a dreary lodging-house. Noticing the grease and dust over everything, he focuses on the once-grand wallpaper:

> The walls were covered with dun-coloured paper, upon which had been printed in oblique reiteration a crimson shape, something of the nature of a curly ostrich feather, or an acanthus flower, that had in its less faded moments a sort of dingy gaiety.
>
> (Ch. 1)

Orwell has similar set-piece descriptions: the furniture in the Brookers' house in *Wigan Pier*; the club billiard-table in *Burmese Days*; the rectory in *A Clergyman's Daughter*; Gordon's room and hideous aspidistra plant in *Keep the Aspidistra Flying*. The past history of the rooms and furniture emphasises their present tawdriness and squalor. These details all underline the theme of loss and decay: the loss of dignity and hope in the Brookers' lodgers; the fall of the Empire; the spiritual and financial poverty of the Anglican Church; the rigid conventions of social class.

In the 1941 essay Orwell attacked Wells chiefly because he disagreed with his optimistic view of the future. Their differences in outlook can be explained largely by the different atmospheres in which they had grown up. Wells had spent his youth in a tranquil time; he tirelessly promoted world peace. Orwell, in contrast, had lived in a period of actual or impending war since his teens. David Lodge has argued that, in spite of his essentially pessimistic view of life, Wells forced optimistic meanings out of his books, that though he tried to confront the difficulty of the private pursuit of happiness in an unjust world, he contrived happy endings: resignation and acceptance of one's ordinary fate, or escape through violence.[26] Orwell seems to have responded to this deeper vein of pessimism. Although Orwell's essay appears to dismiss Wells, as if his influence were no longer useful or relevant, the Wellsian blend of social novel with science fiction (a futuristic social novel) in which the use of technology is a major theme, was to shape *Nineteen Eighty-Four*.

3

Burmese Days: Orwell's Colonial Novel

What lured him to life in the tropic?
Did he venture for fame or for pelf?
Did he seek a career philanthropic?
Or simply to better himself?
But whate'er the temptation that brought him,
Whether piety, dulness, or debts,
He is thine for a price, thou hast bought him,
O Land of Regrets!

Sir Alfred Comyn Lyall, 'The Land of Regrets',
Verses Written in India (1899)

Burmese Days is Orwell's only truly conventional novel. It has two interlocking plots: the main one concerns the hero Flory's courtship of Elizabeth Lackersteen and his moral dilemma about the election of his friend, the Indian Dr Veraswamy, to the European Club; the secondary one describes the plans of U Po Kyin, a prominent Burmese, to be elected to the club himself. Early in the novel Flory claims he is immune to U Po Kyin's schemes, but Kyin disgraces Flory, who loses Elizabeth and kills himself.

Though Orwell uses Flory to express his opposition to British colonial rule, Flory is not an exact self-portrait. We know little about Orwell's life in Burma, except that he was a lonely and efficient policeman. The form of this first novel was undoubtedly shaped by his reading as much as by his experience. The hero and cast of characters, the themes, the plot and its resolution in a catastrophic dénouement, can be traced to the colonial fiction of Kipling, Conrad and Forster. But its personal content and polemic purpose set it apart from other novels of the genre.

43

Burmese Days attempts to come to terms with Orwell's personal history: it expresses (and confesses) shame, self-hatred, frustration and anger. The novel attacks not only colonial rule, but also English education and moral and sexual attitudes.

THEMES AND PATTERNS OF COLONIAL FICTION

The hard-working, lonely Englishman who commits suicide; the young girl sent out from England to find a husband; the manipulative and spying memsahib (the wife of a colonial official); the impossibility of friendship and the disaster of sexual liaisons between black and white, were characters and themes initiated by Kipling.

Kipling's stories contain studies of heroes who work hard in spite of boredom, exhaustion, heat and disease, who long for home in an alien, oppressive landscape. 'Thrown Away', for example, is a story of a too-conscientious young man who cracks under the strain and blows his brains out. 'The Last Relief' tells of a man who throws himself under a train rather than be sent back from leave to almost certain death during a cholera epidemic. In many ways Flory is a typical Kipling hero: he has little money, lives in squalid quarters, eats poor food, drinks heavily and suffers from prickly heat, tropical sores and depression. Though he is a timber merchant, in Burma to make a living rather than serve the Empire, he works in the jungle for weeks on end and copes with sick elephants and broken machinery.

In Kipling's world natives cannot be trusted and white men have to stick together; Indians may be loyal servants but true friendship with them is out of the question. Sexual ties are always doomed. Trejago, the hero of 'Beyond the Pale', is guilty of 'too deep an interest in native life'. As punishment for her affair, her relatives mutilate his mistress, a Hindu widow, and injure him. 'Without Benefit of Clergy' (whose title Orwell later appropriated for his essay on Salvador Dali) describes a happy union between a colonial official, Holden, and a beautiful Indian girl, Ameera. He buys her when she is fourteen, and she bears him a son two years later. Ameera is always fearful of the *mem-log*, white women, her rivals for Holden's love, and he is tortured by guilt about his double life. Eventually he loses both woman and child to disease. In 'Georgie Porgie' the hero buys a lovely

Burmese girl, who tends him and his household perfectly. When he decides to marry and pays her off, she follows him to a new posting in India and wails broken-heartedly when she sees him with his English wife. Orwell follows Kipling in showing that Veraswamy and Ma Hla May suffer as a result of their relationship with Flory, as he does because of his ties to them, but reverses the Kipling idyll of brave white man and submissive, devoted oriental woman. Flory is a coward and Ma Hla May is mercenary and disloyal.

'Bitters Neat' describes another typical Kipling figure, the genteel young woman who seeks a husband in India as an alternative to life as a lady's companion or governess. Her aunt berates her for rejecting a likely suitor, and she is so persecuted by female gossip that she prefers to go home to her fate. Kipling's young women often trap men into romance, distract them from their work and encumber them with responsibilities, while older women are calculating matchmakers, like Mrs Hauksbee, or spiteful and jealous, like the colonel's wife of 'Watches of the Night'. Their memsahibs are part of the colonial official's 'burden'. Mrs Lackersteen and her penniless niece, who passes up a decent suitor (Flory) for a dazzling rogue (Verrall) only to be left with an elderly and unattractive husband (Macgregor), are Kiplingesque characters.

Kipling's stories established colonial fiction as either tales of heroism or social comedies and tragedies. The Anglo-Indian officials, soldiers and merchants view themselves as responsible for creating order and justice in a vast area of darkness and anarchy. Theirs is a closed society, with its own hierarchy and codes of behaviour to which newcomers must adapt, or risk exclusion. In Kipling, the colonial service is a test of manhood. Many of the stories elaborate the theme of his celebrated poem, 'If', which urges the boy to become a man by facing the challenges of life with integrity.

Joseph Conrad, in his novella *Heart of Darkness* (1899), developed the theme of the test of the individual's manhood into a test of the validity of the hero's inner values. Conrad's hero, Marlow, voyages down the Congo in search of Kurtz, a missing Belgian official. He discovers the dying Kurtz, once artistic, intellectual and idealistic, now degraded, corrupt and more primitive than any savage. Marlow's faith in his own civilisation and in his own moral integrity is shaken. When he reports back to

Kurtz's fiancée, he falsifies his account to protect her from such knowledge.

Marlow is the first modern hero of colonial fiction, who questions the basis of European values and temporarily feels estranged from his own culture, but the idea that those at home must be prevented from knowing the truth about colonial life connects him to Kipling's code. In Kipling's 'Thrown Away' the narrator helps a major track down the young suicide. They read his letters to his mother and fiancée and destroy them; they bury him quickly and pretend he has died of cholera. In *Burmese Days* Flory notes the hypocritical inscription on the tombstone of a man who has supposedly died of cholera, but in fact died of drink. To underline the point, rats burrow among the graves. An important motive of colonial fiction, to expose the facts which the official version covers up, was one Orwell incorporated into all his work.

In Kipling the heroism of the survivors in overcoming the challenges of colonial life affirms the superiority of English principles of law and social organisation. Later novelists in the genre (including Forster, Orwell, Joyce Cary and Graham Greene) describe the same predicaments, but they emphasise the corrupting effects of the colonial system on the rulers and the ruled alike, and their heroes, like Conrad's Marlow, question the value of displacing traditional native cultures with Western forms of government and religion. The self-doubting hero of colonial fiction provides the pattern, not only for Flory, torn between obeying his own inner values and the brutal code of the group, but for all of Orwell's subsequent central characters.

E. M. Forster's *A Passage to India*, published ten years before *Burmese Days*, showed Orwell how Kipling characters and themes could be treated ironically. A young Englishwoman, Adela Quested, comes out to India to marry an official. On an excursion organised by a Moslem, Dr Aziz, she accuses the doctor of molesting her. Forster's two contrasting English male characters react in opposite ways to the crisis. Ronny Heaslop, Adela's fiancé and magistrate of Chandrapore, is a young man doing his best to suppress his intelligence and sensitivity in order to conform to the crude manners and prejudiced outlook of his experienced colleagues. Forster uses the reactions of the newly arrived fiancée to reveal how Ronny's limitations are accentuated by his role in India. He has no understanding of Indian religions because 'wherever he entered, mosque, cave or temple, he retained the spiritual outlook of the Fifth Form, and condemned as "weakening" any attempt to understand them' (ch. 28). Although he is honest enough to face the truth when it is revealed, the incident confirms him in his prejudices. Fielding, in contrast, is a middle-aged teacher, a mature and sophisticated intellectual who has Indian friends, respects Indian culture and has no difficulty in disagreeing with his compatriots when Aziz is accused.

Burmese Days uses similar situations – the English girl in search of a husband, a crisis at the club – to reveal character and theme. But Elizabeth is the reverse of Adela: she is pretty, snobbish, cold-hearted and ignorant; Adela is plain, earnest and eager to learn about Indian customs. While Adela is disturbed by Ronny's newly acquired racial superiority, Elizabeth dislikes Flory's independent ideas and wishes he would fit in with the other English. Flory combines aspects of both Ronny and Fielding. Though, like Fielding, he befriends an Indian doctor, appreciates native culture and reads a great deal, he lacks maturity, is very insecure and dreads opposing his countrymen. Flory's agonising dilemma dramatises Orwell's sense of moral compromise in his policeman's job, trapped in a profession which, he felt, led inevitably to self-betrayal. Orwell could never have created a hero like Fielding, an intellectual who is free to change his job and move on, who remains unharmed by the conflict and easily dissociates himself from the other English. Fielding's point of view represents the Bloomsbury left-intellectual position that Orwell detested. In his essay on Kipling Orwell quotes with approval Kipling's line, 'making mock of uniforms which guard you while you sleep' (*CEJL*, 2.187), in order to criticise those who despise the Empire yet enjoy the prosperity it brings.

As in *A Passage to India* the plot of *Burmese Days* turns on two linked crises: Flory's private despair about losing Elizabeth, and the public crisis in race relations, provoked by U Po Kyin. Both novels are set in an isolated community which feels threatened by the native population, during the increasing heat and tension leading up to the monsoon season; the action in both ends in riot and challenge to British order. In both, the conflict in the individual, which concerns a prospective marriage, is put into the perspective of the wider political conflict between two races.

Despite these correspondences, Orwell's novel is very different from Forster's. While Kipling's heroes suffer from overconscientiousness or divided loyalty, they believe in duty and in the work of Empire. Forster's advocate duty to oneself. Orwell's ideal is fidelity both to work and to one's conscience. Although Orwell attacks Kipling throughout the novel, his protagonist resembles a Kipling hero: Flory resents the Burmese who complicate his life and make his job difficult, though he admires the picturesque beauty of native life; he speaks the language and has expertise in his trade and management of his employees; he despises incompetent and ignorant colleagues. Like all of Orwell's central characters, Flory is conscious of living a lie. *Burmese Days* is primarily a study of the corrupting influence of colonialism.

An important theme in Forster, which Orwell takes up, is the harm done by colonial rule to indigenous peoples and cultures.[27] In *A Passage to India* Forster uses Fielding to express the author's view; he devotes considerable space to native characters and settings, because the conflict between British and indigenous culture is central. In contrast, Flory does not represent Orwell's point of view with any consistency, and is as much a victim of the conflict as anyone. Orwell's chief villain is a Burmese, who exploits his people more ruthlessly than the British do. Orwell is far less successful than Forster in creating convincing native characters. U Po Kyin's grotesque obesity and evil plotting make him merely melodramatic; he and his wife speak a faintly archaic formal English which does not suggest Burmese speech very convincingly.[28] Flory asserts that the British are destroying native culture, but he is easily contradicted by Dr Veraswamy, and Flory's charge is not substantiated in the novel. The cultural theme serves largely as local colour: the market, the jungle, the *pwe* dances are the background to Flory's inner struggle, between his private conscience and public behaviour.

THE STRUCTURE OF THE NOVEL: EXPOSITION AND CHARACTERS

The first five chapters of the novel describe one whole day in Kyauktada, effectively sketching a group of distinct characters in a realistic environment, in a specific historical time. Each chapter depicts Flory's character from a different angle. The first mentions him only briefly; the second gives a detailed physical description which emphasises his birthmark and establishes his dissatisfaction with himself and his surroundings. His attempts to hide the disfiguring mark on his face, a symbol of his weakness and vulnerability, give him a 'sidelong', guilty look. Unshaven and hung over from drinking the night before, he calls Kyauktada a 'bloody hole', and is silent or absent while the club members talk. In the third chapter, in conversation with Dr Veraswamy, he explodes with rage and articulates his political views. The fourth chapter describes him at home, in relation to his servants and native mistress, and defines his feelings for Burma and the Burmese. The fifth chapter is partly a biographical essay, explaining how his character has been formed and why he is in this uneasy situation. The chapters increasingly focus on Flory, explain his dilemma and establish some sympathy for him.

The first brief chapter frames the novel by presenting the situation through the eyes of U Po Kyin, a corrupt Burmese magistrate, who manipulates his British masters and now plans to discredit Dr Veraswamy, civil surgeon and superintendent of the jail. He dismisses Flory as a coward. Kyin sets the plot in motion and places Flory and the rest of the British in his malignant perspective. His harsh realism undercuts the self-importance of the characters in the following chapter. Kyin's success suggests that native customs will outlast British order, which is flimsy, superficial and easily subverted by native cunning.

Kipling remarks that it is easy for Anglo-Indians to lose their sense of proportion: in 'that harsh atmosphere men stand out all crude and raw, with nothing to tone them down, and nothing to scale them against' ('Wressley of the Foreign Office', *Plain Tales from the Hills*). Orwell's description, in chapter 2, of the mediocre little town of four thousand inhabitants, artificially created by the British, emphasises its claustrophobic limits, just as the club dialogue conveys the narrow outlook of the members. Initially there are only seven British: Macgregor, the Deputy Commissioner; Westfield, the Superintendent of Police; Maxwell, a forestry officer; Lackersteen, Ellis and Flory, who work for timber companies, and Mrs Lackersteen. The ugly, cramped and dingy club with its 'library' of mildewed volumes, littered magazines and flying beetles is the ironic setting for Ellis's outraged dignity.

All of them except Flory are one-dimensional figures who share the same set of illusions about their racial superiority and self-sacrifice. Macgregor is a satiric type of genial, pompous bureaucrat, repeating the same anecdotes over and over again, speaking in euphemisms or clichés; Westfield is a trigger-happy policeman who leaves his native subordinates to dispense justice; Lackersteen drinks and womanises, and his wife tries to prevent him; Ellis personifies every kind of social prejudice; Maxwell is a foolish young man whose action precipitates the final riot which causes his death. The emphatic agreement of this unattractive group contrasts with Flory's silence and divided loyalty, and Ellis's derision accentuates his weakness.

The conversation which follows Flory's disgusted exit rehearses their grievances, for they are isolated people who console themselves by reinforcing their prejudices. Orwell's period of service coincided with the rise of political protest against British rule in Burma, and he uses this tense period as background for the novel, placing Flory in a specific political situation. Ellis refers to the Amritsar massacre, which occurred in India in 1919, when General Dyer suppressed an illegal gathering by ordering troops to fire into the crowd, and many hundreds were killed or wounded. Dyer was forced to resign, as Mr Macgregor recalls when he calls him 'poor Dyer', and subsequently Indians were granted limited representation in the government and civil service. Such reforms were not immediately extended to Burma, and during Orwell's time there was general hostility to British rule, especially among the university students and Buddhist monks. The club's reaction to the proposed election of a native member is so virulent because they hate the idea of Indians entering the government, and feel threatened by political unrest. Afraid of appearing 'soft' on the natives, they become more and more rigid.

Flory's scene with Veraswamy, which follows in chapter 3, establishes the novel's basic thesis: that colonialism is a form of exploitation, and that those who serve it must be corrupted, either by exerting their power, or by living a secret life of ideological disagreement. Like the discussion in the previous chapter, this conversation is habitual, it 'took place as often as the two men met', and expresses frustration and anger. Flory's views generally contradict those expressed in the club. He uses Kipling's tags bitterly ('slimy white man's burden humbug') while Macgregor uses them approvingly ('cares of Empire'). In an ironic reversal of roles, the Indian asserts his faith in British law, justice, trade and progress, while the Briton deplores the theft of resources, the suppression of native industries, the destruction of culture and the introduction of disease. Flory hates most the hypocritical pretence that the British are there to do good (contradicting, though not to her face, Mrs Lackersteen's comments in the previous chapter). This argument reflects an ambivalence about colonialism which the novel does not resolve: the doctor, a man of science, argues for the pragmatic benefits of hygiene and rational order, while Flory expresses Orwell's cynicism about Western notions of progress and his revulsion from 'the dirty work of Empire'.

Though Veraswamy is a Kiplingesque type of good-native-as-loyal-servant ('his face, with dark liquid eyes, recalled that of a black retriever dog' – ch. 2) his situation contributes to the criticism of colonialism in the novel. An isolated immigrant, like the British he is deceived by his Burmese subordinates, who undo his work. At the same time he is despised by the British and betrayed by Flory, who uses him as a sounding board for the things he dare not say out loud at the club. Veraswamy is the only decent person in the novel, and the only one Flory can talk to. Yet their cultural and temperamental differences divide them, reveal the limits of Veraswamy's understanding and accentuate Flory's intellectual and emotional isolation. The conversation increases Flory's frustration as it emphasises his discontent. It leaves him doubly guilty: disloyal to his own people and country, and disloyal to his friend.

Orwell's portrayal of master–servant relationships throughout the novel is observant, satiric and poignant: the politeness of the club servants contrasts with the rudeness of their masters, who do not approve of them speaking English correctly; Ellis is outraged when Verrall kicks the butler, partly because he regards kicking the butler as *his* prerogative, and partly because he is afraid of appearing to disapprove of such treatment; Maxwell's death is truly mourned only by his servants and forest ranger.

Flory's relationships with his servant Ko S'la and his mistress Ma Hla May reveal his relative immaturity, his lack of self-confidence, his physical and moral inertia. Though Ko S'la is the same age as his master, thirty-five, he has two wives and several children, and still regards the bachelor Flory as a boy, to whom he feels tender and protective. Later, when Flory falls from Verrall's horse, Ko S'la chides him, calling him too old for such risky games. Flory is thus both old and young, without the advantages of youth or age. Orwell uses ironic contrast to suggest Flory's guilt about having a servant perform intimate, menial services for him. Tending to a stupefied and humiliated Flory, Ko S'la addresses him reverentially as 'holy one', and 'the god'. Flory is also guilty about Ma Hla May, whom he literally owns. But her beauty is alien, she has no affection for him, and uses him in her turn to acquire status and money. Sex with her fills him with shame and increases his loneliness.

After the sordid encounter with her in chapter 4, Flory walks several miles into the jungle and bathes in a clear pool, a cleansing ritual which temporarily washes away his guilt. A peasant gives him a ride on a cart back to a nearby village, where he is given tea and admires the colourful, tranquil scene. Flory is courteous to the peasants and sensitive to natural beauty. His instinctive return to the natural world, where he becomes newly aware of his loneliness, suggests that he is a soiled Adam who wants to be redeemed by an Eve, the wife he hopes can help him start afresh in Burma and make his life a paradise.

This peaceful mood is shattered by his evening visit to the club, in chapter 5, where he feigns agreement with Ellis and Westfield and signs their insulting letter refusing to admit a native member. As if to explain his cowardice and passivity, Orwell then gives us an overview of Flory's life up to this point. His weak character is said to originate in his ugly birthmark, which caused him to be victimised at school. These experiences made him fear being an outsider and yearn to belong and be accepted. In time he learned to victimise others, to despise the intellect, to lie and play football; he left school 'a barbarous young lout'. His youth in Burma has been spent in work, sports, drinking and rare bouts of fornication, thinking neither of the past nor the future; he has not been home for fifteen years, his youth is gone and his health damaged. But Flory's problem is that, despite his efforts to fit in, he has developed a 'hatred of the atmosphere of imperialism in which he lived', in 'the stifling, stultifying world' where 'every white man is a cog in the wheels of despotism' and 'free speech is unthinkable'. Like Winston Smith in *Nineteen Eighty-Four*, Flory pretends to share the assumptions of his social group, but is consumed by a secret desire to rebel. His visits to the club re-enact the situation at school: there is no intimacy, yet no privacy; Flory feels compelled to follow the 'pukka sahibs' code', just as he had at school.

In 1936, in a review of a colonial novel (*CEJL*, 1.234), Orwell defined the theme of 'double homesickness' that he himself had developed earlier in this chapter of *Burmese Days*: expatriates long for years to go home, but when they return feel piercing regret for the country they have left. Like a Kipling hero, in the past Flory has had his leave cancelled and has to replace a dead colleague. He has discovered his attachment to Burma and its people, but over the years has lost his British identity, and now feels more cut off than ever; his emotional ties trap him rather than sustain him.

FLORY AND ELIZABETH: THE SEXUAL THEME IN THE COLONIAL SETTING

The suffocating beauty of the Burmese jungle emphasises Flory's ambivalent attitude to the country. It is both heaven and hell. The Miltonic theme of paradise lost is suggested in chapter 4, where Flory laments his isolation: 'Alone, alone, the bitterness of being alone!' In chapter 5 Flory repeats his need for a companion (and Elizabeth duly appears in chapter 6). In chapter 15, as he is about to propose, he assures her Burma could be a 'paradise if one weren't alone'. Elizabeth, however, is an ironic Eve. Although she is young and sexually innocent, she already shares the corrupt values of this Eden; she is as eager to fit in with the club as Flory is to reject it.

All their encounters are ironic. Flory is desperate to confess his guilty desire *not* to be a pukka sahib, but the more he talks, the more alarmed and disgusted Elizabeth becomes. Though they are first brought together in the Lawrentian scenes when he 'rescues' her from the bullocks and takes her out shooting, their conversations show how far apart they are, intellectually and emotionally. When he first kisses her Flory feels most remote from her, and his passionate speech contrasts with her trivial thoughts. As he tries to tell her about his utter loneliness, the uncomprehending Elizabeth merely thinks that perhaps he'd be less lonely if he had a radio. For her, marriage to Flory is just a means of escape: first from poverty in Europe, then from her uncle's advances, and lastly from humiliation at Verrall's departure.

Orwell's novels frequently describe the same sexual relationship: the female, like Elizabeth, is sexually fearful and inhibited; the male, like Flory, lonely and frustrated, desires the woman but is resentful of her power to withhold her love. In *Burmese Days* Orwell uses the colonial setting and theme of cultural conflict to probe this sexual theme. As Forster does in *A Passage to India*, Orwell uses the capacity to appreciate native culture as a measure of character. In a series of scenes in which Flory tries to introduce Elizabeth to Burmese life and allow her to share his love of the place and people, Elizabeth reveals her hostility to all ordinary sexuality. She finds the traditional dances disgusting and is outraged when a naked baby urinates on a shop floor; on both occasions she insults their native hosts.

The Eurasians, Francis and Samuel, disturb her because they are living proof of sexual union between black and white. Far from sympathising with their anomalous position, she instinctively snubs them. Elizabeth believes in white superiority, that racial mixtures produce 'degenerates' who should somehow be got rid of, and that only 'low' whites have sexual relations with people of colour. Flory's gentle, mocking contradictions disturb her even more. He points out that many more people on earth are brown than white, that physical differences between races are negligible, and that Francis and Samuel were fathered by English clergymen. Elizabeth is so alarmed by his unorthodox remarks that he suppresses his kindly instincts towards the Eurasians and cuts the conversation short.

Elizabeth's remark that 'only a very low kind of man would ... have anything to do with native women' revives Flory's guilt about his sexual life. He has jilted a Eurasian girl in Mandalay; he worries about what will become of Ma Hla May when he drives her away. When Elizabeth rejects and humiliates him he continues to court her because, like Kipling's Georgie Porgie, he wants the security of marriage to one of his own kind. Even when he realises that she is 'silly, snobbish, heartless' (ch. 20), he still longs for her and regards her as his last chance to make his life in Burma bearable.

Despite some hostile authorial comment, Orwell gives us enough detail about Elizabeth's life and circumstances to allow her some sympathy. In her attempt to escape genteel poverty, youth and good looks are her only assets. She must marry, but social and sexual codes demand that she be passive; she cannot complain about her uncle (her only alternative to staying with him would be to go home); she cannot approach Verrall directly, nor complain about his behaviour. Her aunt (whose own marriage is an ironic example of Elizabeth's goal) is so eager to get rid of her that she shamelessly switches allegiance from Flory to Verrall and back to Flory. Since Elizabeth has to keep up appearances at all costs (she insists on calling him 'Mr Flory', as if to deny their intimacy), Flory's disgrace in the club and at the church finally destroys his chances of marrying her, in spite of Verrall's defection.

The sexual triangle (or square, if we include Ma Hla May) is rather subtle.[29] Ma Hla May and Verrall are both coldly exploitive, while Elizabeth and Flory are victims of romantic illusion, and are punished by the outcome of the novel. In strong contrast to Flory, Elizabeth and Verrall are described in Lawrentian terms: young, blond, healthy animals, handsome, anti-intellectual, with an affinity for horses and the crueller sports. Unlike Flory, an obsessive talker, Verrall barely speaks unless to give orders or insults. Offensive and irresponsible, he evades disgrace while Flory courts disaster; his confident good looks make Flory acutely conscious of his disfiguring mark. Verrall is a stereotypical cad, but he has an important role in the argument of the novel.[30] He is at the social apex of the pyramid of British officials, and, though they loathe him, he represents upper-class glamour and power. Ellis's vile tongue, so potent a weapon against Flory, is powerless against Verrall. His savage egotism is another contradiction of the myth that the colonialist works to civilise a primitive people.

FLORY AND THE NARRATOR

The title of *Burmese Days* ironically suggests the complacent memoir of an old India hand. In Evelyn Waugh's *Put Out More Flags* (1942) a publisher describes such a book: 'Met old So-and-so at the club. Got button-holed. Fellow's just retired from Malay States. Written his reminiscences. We shall have to do them for him.'[31] *Burmese Days*, however, angrily repudiates both Kipling's imperialist doctrine and Forster's liberal ethos. At the same time, as the title suggests, the novel *is* in part a fictionalised memoir, which vents Orwell's anger about his education, his training and function in Burma.

Richard Hoggart has said that Orwell's self-characterisation in *Wigan Pier* suggests 'a very vulnerable man, and an obsessively *driven* man, a man with at times a burning sacrificial egoism'.[32] This could describe Flory equally well; his loneliness makes him vulnerable; although he tries to hide his contempt for the colonial system, he is driven by guilt to confess it; he is obsessed with self-loathing and ends his life in literal self-sacrifice. In *Wigan Pier* Orwell describes the landscape of Burma as a nightmare and the writing of *Burmese Days* an attempt to exorcise it (ch. 7). Flory is a negative self-portrait in which Orwell imagines, as in a bad dream, what life might have been like had he gone back there.

While Orwell's close identification with the central character gives the novel emotional intensity, his ambivalent attitude towards him creates problems of tone, form and meaning. The novel is narrated in the third person, chiefly from the central character's point of view; but the narrator both sympathises with and also strongly disapproves of Flory, and sees the benefits of British rule as clearly as its injustices. Shifts in point of view and confusion between the narrative voice and Flory's inner thoughts and speech blur the meaning.

Chapter 2 presents Flory sympathetically. The scene in the club reveals the petty snobbery and racial attitudes he loathes. But the narrator also explains and excuses the British mentality by emphasising the hardships of the club members' lives; the jeering yellow faces of the high-school boys; the discomforts of their camps, offices and bungalows; the hardships of the diet and the climate. In chapter 5, after analysing Flory's misery and hatred of his compatriots at some length, the narrator once again intervenes to characterise colonials as 'a dull, decent people, cherishing and fortifying their dullness behind a quarter of a million bayonets'; they are essentially unheroic and untalented, but no worse than anyone else. Though such rhetorical 'fairness' has its place in an argument, it detracts from the sympathetic portrait of Flory that the narrative is constructing. The logic of the narrator's commentary seems to suggest that Macgregor's hypocrisy and Ellis's racial hatred are normal and Flory's unease pathological.

Thus far the narrative seems to waver between endorsing Flory's views and opposing them, but then the narrative tone changes from essay-like objectivity to a fierce tirade from Flory's point of view, as if the narrator and Flory are one: 'you are free to be a drunkard . . . but you are not free to think for yourself'. Flory goes on at length, describing experiences he remembers with shame ('You see louts fresh from school kicking grey-haired servants') and clearly these experiences are shared by the narrator. Both the narrator and Flory make frequent satiric literary allusions (especially to Shakespeare), a verbal signal which tends to link them further.

The early chapters describe Flory's spiritual crisis in such a way that we might reasonably expect him to resolve it, but his weakness of character is exaggerated and the plot manipulated to disappoint this expectation. Flory theoretically has a choice: he can either get out of the system by leaving Burma, or he can create his own world within it. Since he cannot leave, because he now feels Burma is his home, he must try to accommodate himself, and he courts Elizabeth as a way to do this. Although he realises that she cannot agree with his views, he pursues her, loses his integrity, despairs and kills himself.

Flory's passivity and moral timidity are inconsistent with the spiritual and intellectual awareness described in the early chapters. Though cynical about politics and sceptical about others' motives, Flory is naïve and sees everything in terms of his own personal guilt. When Elizabeth turns him down because he is 'keeping a Burmese woman', his reaction is self-loathing, the sense that he has 'dirtied himself beyond redemption', and he is haunted by a vision of all the women in his past (ch. 17). Just as he passively endorses Ellis's racial views, so he accepts Elizabeth's narrow-minded and irrelevant morality, and makes no attempt to defend himself. The plot delays Flory's actions, while U Po Kyin's machinations proceed unchecked. He fails to kiss Elizabeth on their first hunt; his first proposal is interrupted by an earthquake, his second prevented by Verrall's arrival, which prompts Mrs Lackersteen to tell Elizabeth about Flory's mistress.

Orwell constructs the story of Flory's life on a Kiplingesque model; Flory commits suicide under stress and his death is disguised as an accident. But Flory does not completely fail the test of colonial life. In fact he makes quite a success of it, in spite of his brutalising education and environment. He is not destroyed by Burma: he is doomed from the start. Flory is decent and humane, but his failure results from a weak character, of which the birthmark is the obvious symbol, the reason not only for his social failures, but for his moral cowardice as well. As Elizabeth reflects, 'it was, finally, the birthmark that had damned him' (ch. 24). The novel begins by attacking colonialism, but ends by attacking Flory. Flory's weakness undermines Orwell's anti-colonialist arguments.

It is interesting to compare the clarity and conviction of Orwell's two essays on Burma with the ultimately blurred effect of *Burmese Days*. 'A Hanging' (1931) describes witnessing an execution and the narrator's realisation of the 'unspeakable wrongness' of cutting a life short (*CEJL*, 1.45). 'Shooting an Elephant' (1936), also narrated in the first person, describes an episode where Orwell is called upon to shoot a rogue elephant which has killed a man. When he finally catches up with it a huge crowd has assembled, and the elephant is no longer dangerous. He has to shoot it, however, because his audience expects it and he would look foolish if he did not. Because he cannot risk being laughed at, he does something he considers wrong. The point of the essay is that 'when the white man turns tyrant it is his own freedom that he destroys' (*CEJL*, 1.239). Both essays clearly articulate the theme that 'in order to rule over barbarians, you have to become one' (*CEJL*, 1.235). Police work reveals the colonial official's moral dilemma in its clearest form, because the policeman must act, whether or not he is sure that what he is doing is right. In the essays the narrator's actions and reactions demonstrate fully exactly how the possession of such power forces him to follow a collective ethos, rather than personal judgement.

Perhaps if Orwell had made his central character a policeman or administrator the moral hazards of Flory's position would have been more dramatic. In Joyce Cary's *Mister Johnson* (1939), the hero is a District Officer who must personally execute his loyal but criminal clerk; in Graham Greene's *The Heart of the Matter* (1948), the hero, a Police Commissioner who becomes corrupted, betrays his loyal servant and causes his murder. Both of these novels share Orwell's general theme of the corrupting effects of colonialism on the rulers and the ruled, but express it more clearly through the central character.

Orwell's attack on colonialism is diluted in part because he divided aspects of his life and character into three, instead of creating one character to embody all the contradictions of his experience in Burma. He gives Flory sympathetic qualities: book-ishness, loneliness, moral and political awareness, appreciation of the Burmese people and their way of life; he gives shameful ideas and behaviour to Westfield and Ellis.

These men express the irritation and concern to keep up appearances that the narrator describes in 'Shooting an Elephant'. Though Westfield 'loathed running in these poor devils of common thieves' (ch. 6), he is more concerned with the appearance than the reality of justice. Like Ellis, he wants revenge for Maxwell's death, but believes they had better 'hang wrong fellow than no fellow' so as not to lose face (ch. 22). The episode where Ellis strikes a schoolboy across the eyes is a crueller version of a real incident in Orwell's life. In 1924, going down to a platform in a Rangoon railway station, Orwell was tripped by a schoolboy and fell heavily down the stairs. He furiously raised his cane to strike the boy's head but hit him across the back instead. Once on the packed train he had to face the anger of a crowd of schoolboys and students.[33] Orwell exaggerates Ellis's rage and cruelty (the boys provoke him merely by grinning at him) to dramatise the white man's tension, his fear of looking a fool, and his abuse of his power. But Ellis's response is unreasonable, and the results extreme (the boy becomes blind), while in the real-life incident Orwell's surprise and angry reaction are understandable.[34]

Though Flory's attempt to re-form his own character and understand his social role is moving, he is a self-punishing, limited person of mediocre talents, unable to set himself free from a stifling environment. Orwell's fictional characters tend to be representative types, rather than complex or exceptional people. Influenced by his reading of nineteenth-century novels, Orwell assumed that plot and characters should be neatly tied up at the end. These novelistic habits make for pessimistic, foregone conclusions.[35] The average man may have stirrings of revolt, but in practice rarely changes his life. At the end of *Burmese Days* the evil U Po Kyin and bureaucratic Macgregor achieve their aims, and Flory's finer feelings end in death.

4

A Clergyman's Daughter: Orwell's Experimental Novel

> The trivial round, the common task
> Will furnish all we ought to ask.
>
> John Keble, *The Christian Year*[36]

In January 1934 Orwell went to live with his parents in South-wold, to recover from the pneumonia which had forced him to resign his teaching job. Here he worked on *A Clergyman's Daughter*, which he completed by October. Since his return from Burma and Paris he had gone tramping and hop-picking, had briefly slept out on the streets and had even been arrested. He had written essays about these experiences and now tried to combine documentary and autobiographical essays with fiction.

Late in 1932 Orwell managed to borrow a copy of Joyce's *Ulysses*, then banned in Great Britain. He studied the novel intently, and wrote several perceptive and enthusiastic letters about it to his friends over the next two years, while working on *A Clergyman's Daughter*. He particularly valued the way the novel seemed to sum up 'the fearful despair that is almost normal in modern times' (*CEJL*, 1.21). Though he admitted that reading *Ulysses* had given him 'an inferiority complex' (*CEJL*, 1.39), because he realised that he was incapable of Joyce's dazzling word-play and poetic, allusive style, Orwell tried to imitate the form of *Ulysses*, a novel structured on the wanderings of a central character and narrated in various prose styles. He used Dorothy Hare's experiences to link the documentary and fictional material together, and directly imitated a chapter from *Ulysses* in the central section of his own book.

A Clergyman's Daughter is only intermittently experimental. Its nineteenth-century design is centred on a woman's struggle to

60

live with, in the words of George Eliot, 'no coherent social faith and order' to sustain her. Dorothy suffers from the humanist dilemma: the problem of how to live honourably without religious belief. She loses her way, both materially and morally, and, instead of discovering her own values, doggedly returns to duty.

PLOT AND STRUCTURE

Divided into five long chapters, the novel begins in the satiric mode of *Burmese Days*. Like Flory, Dorothy is anxious, unhappy and overworked, about to suffer a spiritual and emotional crisis. In chapter 2, a fictionalised documentary, she goes tramping and hop-picking. She becomes destitute and is arrested for begging at the end of chapter 3, which is written as a surrealistic play. Chapter 4 returns to a conventional third-person narrative, with didactic digressions, to describe her life as a teacher. The final chapter reverts to the characters, setting and style of the first. The conclusion attempts to resolve Dorothy's early crisis by summarising her response to the disparate experiences described in the novel.

Orwell realised that he had not been entirely successful in blending the fictional and non-fictional elements in this book. 'It was a good idea', he wrote, with some exaggeration, to his agent, 'but I am afraid I have made a muck of it.' He acknowledged that 'it is very disconnected as a whole, and rather unreal' (*CEJL*, 1.141). Orwell's basic problem is that he chooses a central character with a very limited range of experience. In the first chapter he places Dorothy in a vivid physical and social setting. But, in order to make her life include his own recent experiences, Orwell has to make her leave home. She is a passive person, someone to whom things happen rather than one who acts on those around her. Orwell manoeuvres her into each new situation, relying on mechanical plot-devices and stereotyped characters, which not only violate the novel's initial realistic mode but also conflict with the documentary material of chapters 2 and 4.

Since no one of Dorothy's background voluntarily risks destitution, she rather improbably suffers amnesia. The days between her disappearance from the rectory and her recovery of consciousness in New Kent Road are not explained. She meets Nobby and his friends by coincidence. When she realises her true identity she does not go to the police, but out of extreme diffidence and fear of scandal keeps her assumed name and writes a letter to her father. His lack of response, though in character, is necessary to complete Dorothy's degradation. Twice she is rescued by an external agent, first by her cousin Tom Hare (an elderly version of P. G. Wodehouse's Bertie Wooster, complete with Jeeves-like manservant), who arranges her teaching job. In spite of her ill-treatment at the hands of Mrs Creevy, Dorothy does not leave until she is thrown out. Finally Warburton, her middle-aged suitor from chapter 1, acts as a Dickensian benefactor and takes her home. Dorothy can now return because Mrs Semprill, the gossip responsible for spreading the scandal that Dorothy has eloped, has been sued for libel by another victim and has left town.

Orwell attempts to give the rambling novel some unity and Dorothy's adventures the illusion of reality by correlating the action with the passage of time. She leaves home in high summer, spends the harvest time picking hops in Kent, stays a week at 'Mary's', a cheap brothel and lodging-house, sleeps in Trafalgar Square for ten days and spends another ten days with her uncle. She goes to Ringwood Academy some time in October, after the term has begun, and stays there two terms. She returns to Knype in April, and soon starts making costumes for the summer pageant, her previous occupation.

CHAPTER 1: THE SOCIOLOGY OF SETTING

Like *Burmese Days*, *A Clergyman's Daughter* begins with a satiric portrait of a town and its inhabitants, here based on Orwell's observation of Southwold and his parents' social world. Knype Hill, representative of 'the most class-ridden country in the world' (*CEJL*, 2.67), has three social strata. Apart from its local aristocrat and petty gentry, the upper layer consists of the well-off members of the Conservative Club, whose womenfolk frequent Ye Olde Tea Shoppe. Mr Blifil-Gordon, a nouveau-riche parliamentary candidate, is a newcomer.[37] The middle layer are small shopkeepers, tradesmen and teachers, the bottom are the newly arrived factory workers, who make up more than half the population of the town; live-in domestic workers, like the Hares' servant, Ellen; and the rural labourers, like Mr and Mrs Pither, the poorest of all. Dorothy's parish visits and fund-raising schemes are typical of the work done at this period, often by single women, to help the poor. Very little public assistance existed.

Ironically, however, Dorothy herself is materially not much better off than those she helps. The Hares belong to the impoverished section of the professional middle class who cling to their respectability and regard themselves as socially superior to people who often live better than they do. The High Street in Knype was 'one of those sleepy, old-fashioned streets that look so ideally peaceful on a casual visit and so very different when ... you have a creditor behind every window'. Dorothy's social situation suggests an idea Orwell developed later in *Wigan Pier*: that, although old class divisions still existed, economic changes were levelling the middle class down, and this group had much to gain by aligning itself politically with the working class.

George Bowling in *Coming Up for Air* recalls the smell of the church of his boyhood as 'death and life mixed up together', yet feels even that corpse-like air was fresher than the menacing atmosphere of 1939. But there is no nostalgia in Orwell's description of St Athelstan's. Its physical condition symbolises the death of Christianity itself. A half-empty ruin, riddled with dry-rot, its unswung bells threaten to smash through the belfry and crush the congregation. Repairs can never be made, since like the Rector himself the church is heavily in debt. The younger son of a younger son of a baronet, cold, snobbish and rigid, the Rector has neglected all but his formal duties, alienated his parishioners, never tried to attract new members from the mass of factory workers and refused to adapt to popular taste in worship. All the gentry, except the decaying Miss Mayfill, and most of the prosperous middle class, have left his church. The Rector loathes the present because he has lost status and security; in another age he would have been a contented scholar with a sinecure. He lives in 'the age of Lenin and the *Daily Mail*' but chooses to ignore it and remain in the past, denying his debts, his stock-market losses, his dwindling capital and congregation.

In his poem 'A Happy Vicar I Might Have Been', Orwell imagined himself as a nineteenth-century clergyman and contrasted the emotional security of that life with the uncertainty of the present. He quoted it in his autobiographical 'Why I Write' to explain his own blend of conservative and radical impulses. The melancholy description of the Rector's empty church (complete with the axe-marks of a previous social revolution) expresses regret at the passing of a traditional way of life.

DOROTHY AND THE THEME OF FAITH

Like Flory in *Burmese Days* and Winston Smith in *Nineteen Eighty-Four*, Dorothy is a weak, guilt-ridden person who loses confidence in the value of her work and the code of her class. Orwell rather crudely highlights symbolic events to chart her gradual loss of faith. At first she goads herself with petty punishments to complete the menial tasks ahead; when she regains consciousness she has lost the gold cross from her neck; when her father fails to answer her letter she discovers that she can no longer pray.

Critics have noted that Orwell does not portray Dorothy's loss of faith convincingly.[38] There are two reasons for this. First, Orwell was more interested in the social effects of dwindling Christian faith than the individual's sense of loss.[39] Secondly, Orwell fails to maintain Dorothy's consciousness as the controlling point of view in the novel. In chapter 2 her actions and feelings are summarised rather externally. Despite the detailed information we are given about her life, Dorothy remains primarily a type, one of the spinsters bicycling to church, a feature of the landscape Orwell described in *The Lion and the Unicorn* (*CEJL*, 2.57).

All Dorothy's contacts with Christians are profoundly depressing: her father is cruelly indifferent; the sexton, Proggett, is stupidly devoted to the church building; old Mrs Pither's naïve belief in heaven contrasts absurdly with her foul living conditions; Victor Stone is obsessed with sterile disputes in the *Church Times*. Dorothy is repelled by Mrs Mayfill's wet lips and Mrs Pither's knotted veins. In Trafalgar Square she meets a defrocked clergyman who mocks Christian worship; in Mrs Creevy's school she confronts a rigid nonconformist mentality which reduces religion to a set of prohibitions. The novel does not attack religion itself, for those without religion are equally discredited: Mrs Creevy for her love of money, Mr Warburton for his pursuit of pleasure.

Dorothy is a type of Victorian heroine, sexless, anxious and victimised. She carries an enormous practical and social burden: the housekeeping, cleaning the church, visiting the sick, organising women's groups, children's plays and jumble sales; yet she receives nothing in return. Dorothy acts as a surrogate for her father in the parish, and on her travels explores the ugly realities that he and his class deny.

Orwell modernises his sexless heroine by providing a Lawrentian explanation for her emotional strain. Just as Flory's birthmark has destroyed his self-confidence, so Dorothy has a 'special defect', her secret dread of men, an 'incurable disability that she carried through life'. Five years before the novel opens she has refused marriage to a decent man, and escape from her father's house. Dorothy has witnessed 'dreadful scenes' during her parents' unhappy marriage. She associates sex with male oppression ('men touch you – maul you about'), denies her own sexuality, deliberately takes cold baths and dresses dowdily. When she kisses the fennel in the meadow (another Lawrentian touch) she reveals her repressed longing for physical contact, but she hastily punishes herself for 'nature-worship'. Warburton's advances revive her anxiety and she feels revolted by the close-up sight and smell of him.[40]

Dorothy is the most extreme example of the distaste for and unhappiness about sex which is common in Orwell's characters. Orwell agreed with D. H. Lawrence that the education and upbringing of his time repressed sexual feeling and made it 'a dirty little secret' (in Lawrence's phrase) which could poison one's life. In Lawrence's novels sexual union can be a means of achieving that community of feeling and purpose lacking in society as a whole. But Warburton is no Lawrentian hero, and Dorothy's final scene with him shows that she cannot escape her isolation in a sexual relationship. She finds nothing to compensate for the loss of religious faith.

CHAPTER 2: THE ESCAPE INTO POVERTY

In chapter 2 Dorothy's mental suffering takes second place to physical hardship. She learns 'the peculiar, blowsy, witless feeling that came of sleeplessness and constant exposure to the air'. Now poorer than any of those she used to visit in Knype, she joins Nobby in begging or stealing from middle-class people, and learns how to do exhausting work which provides just enough money to survive. She stands out from the rest of the pickers not only by her education, but also by her awareness of the existence of a life beyond this endless round of work or search for food and shelter. Her problem is 'puzzling out her identity', but even after she regains her memory she wanders between the worlds of the haves and have-nots, and belongs to neither. She learns from her fruitless search for a housekeeping job (in chapter 3) that, when you are homeless and jobless, your previous social position counts for nothing. Orwell uses Dorothy's rapid descent into destitution to emphasise a key idea in the novel: the precariousness of security, the nearness of poverty, for many people in England during the 1930s.

As his essay 'Hop Picking' shows, Orwell had learned the custom of pairing-off to survive the rigours of tramping. His mate Ginger is the model for Nobby, whose resourceful petty crimes keep Dorothy going. Unlike in chapter 1, Dorothy is consistently helped by those she meets. When she enters the camp she sees 'ragged, agreeable-looking people' cooking their dinners over fires. She stumbles exhausted into the women's tent, and an anonymous woman helps her into a sack to keep warm. A cockney couple, the Turles, give them food, tactfully saying it is left over. Her need for work and survival leads her to form new social ties, and even obliterates her sexual fears. When Nobby is arrested she is glad to work with Deafie, the tramp who obsessively shows off his penis.

The style of chapter 2 shows many signs of its origin in 'Hop Picking'. The narrative continues to describe Dorothy's thoughts and feelings, but slips into an autobiographical essay mode, as in *Burmese Days*. When he describes Dorothy picking hops Orwell uses the impersonal 'you' instead of 'she': 'the work took hold of you and absorbed you. It was stupid work, mechanical, exhausting and every day more painful to the hands, and yet you never wearied of it' because it is outdoor, communal work.

He expresses a general conclusion about Dorothy's experience of tramping in impersonal terms, rather than in terms of her particular character: 'In such circumstances one can only keep alive if one hunts for food as persistently and single-mindedly as a wild beast.' Orwell uses this objective, essay style to convey much detailed information about the language and habits of tramps, cockneys and gypsies, and the procedures, conditions and wages of hop-picking. But these facts are included for their intrinsic interest rather than for their utility in advancing the story or illuminating the theme.

In chapter 2 the characterisation changes no less than the style. In chapter 1 the characters are portrayed satirically, in their particular environment, and we perceive them through Dorothy's more complex consciousness. In chapter 2 the characters – based on the people Orwell met on the road and hop-picking – Nobby, Deafie, the Turles, Mrs McElligot the old Irishwoman, all come to life briefly and anecdotally in the routine of work or search for food and shelter. Mrs McElligot's account in chapter 3 of how she once slept curled up close to a sow in a pigsty is one of many such stories from his essays that Orwell weaves into the novel.

CHAPTER 3: ORWELL'S JOYCEAN EXPERIMENT

Orwell maintains continuity in chapter 3 by using many of the characters from the previous chapter. The vagrants from the hop-fields are now sleeping out in the first cold autumn nights in Trafalgar Square. Here Orwell returns to the themes of chapter 1, but switches styles once more, imitating the technique of the 'nighttown' episode in Joyce's *Ulysses*. In this late section of Joyce's long novel, his protagonist Leopold Bloom pursues and rescues Stephen Dedalus, a bitter, anti-clerical young man who is being led drunkenly through Dublin's brothel district. The action is patterned on the episode in the *Odyssey* where Ulysses and his men land on the island of Circe, an enchantress who turns the sailors to swine. Joyce uses dramatic form, including stage directions, and an array of real characters, some particular to this episode, some from earlier chapters of the novel, as well as others who are apparitions from Bloom's and Stephen's past lives.

Orwell tries to convey Dorothy's state of mind by imitating Joyce's counterpoint of voices and accumulation of disconnected, trivial or apparently pointless speeches, which nevertheless relate to the plot and theme of the novel. The disparate scraps of dialogue, part real, part dream, evoke the social, sexual and religious motifs of the first chapter.

Orwell uses his documentary observations to create a surreal scene. The grotesque group attempt to make tea, keep warm and get to sleep. Their doze is interrupted by a policeman, who tries to move them on. Eventually they go to a café which opens at five, where they share cups of tea and sleep on the tabletops. A short narrative of Dorothy's arrest for begging, based on Orwell's essay 'Clink', ends the chapter. The down-and-out have a rough camaraderie: they make tea by 'bumming' water, tea and sugar, and use a filthy can of evaporated milk, eventually plunging their fingers into the can to get the last drops; they squeeze together and wrap themselves in newspaper posters to keep warm. The dialogue, enlivened by colourful and ironic rhyming slang, reveals their courage and vitality: 'consultation-free' (= tea), 'money-or-your-life' (= knife), 'nine-carat-gold' (= cold).

Though all the characters pursue an inner reverie, their speeches share a common theme: the loss of security and happiness. Mrs Wayne recalls her mother's china tea-service; Mrs McElligot misses Michael, her tramp partner; Mrs Bendigo (who belies her name, which suggests benediction, or blessing) curses her unfaithful husband; Nosey Watson swears revenge on his mates, who have betrayed him. Marriage and the security of the family are recurring motifs. Ginger repeatedly sings an envious song of the happy girl and boy 'in their joy', while Mr Tallboys recites part of the marriage-service. Dorothy is urged to get close to old 'Daddy', who smells foul and is 'chatty' (lousy), but is warm, an ironic contrast to her own cold father. Deafie's repeated obsessive line ('*With* my willy willy –') suggests both the sexual aspect of men Dorothy fears, and also the social isolation of the tramp who, like Dorothy, has no possibility of a conventional sexual or family life.

Mr Tallboys, the defrocked rector, is the strongest, most insistent voice in the chapter. He says, in Latin, 'I am not what I was in the reign of King Edward' and later adds, 'et ego in Crockford'[41] – that is, he was once listed in the clerical directory. Mr Tallboys' regret for his past status and comfort, his contempt for his parishioners, his pride in his surplices and skill at chanting parody Mr Hare's attitudes. He mocks Dorothy by alluding to 'spinsters growing bony and desperate' and to the newspaper headlines about the sexual affairs which lost him his job: 'Missing Canon's Sub Rosa Romance', which ironically recall the false rumours about Dorothy's disappearance.[42] Mr Tallboys recites hymns, psalms, blasphemous prayers and finally a Black Mass, echoing the scene in nighttown in *Ulysses*, where Stephen participates in a Black Mass. Orwell's Joycean imitation strikes a false note here, because Dorothy's loss of faith is an altogether milder experience than Joyce's passionate repudiation of Catholicism. Dorothy's loss represents a wider social breakdown, rather than a fierce inner struggle.

In chapter 1 Dorothy worries about the poor of the parish, but her anguish is primarily a spiritual malaise. In chapters 2 and 3 she suffers so much physically that she no longer needs jabs with a pin to mortify herself. The tramps in the square enact an absurd comedy of suffering, wrapping themselves 'with infinite difficulty' in 'a monstrous cocoon of paper'. Dorothy remarks that 'It's so absurd that one wouldn't believe it if one didn't know it was true', emphasising an important idea in the novel: that the middle-class do not know, and could not imagine, the misery of the underclass. The form of the chapter as a whole suggests that Orwell realised that the experience of destitution was more fantastic than anything he could invent, and that the conventional novel form was inadequate to express it.

CHAPTER 4: ORWELL'S ESSAY ON EDUCATION

In part an autobiographical and didactic essay on teaching, this chapter is plotted like a Dickens novel. Dorothy is rescued from the gutter and restored to respectability at Ringwood Academy, but discovers she is still subject to 'the mysterious power of money'. Fearful of losing her identity once more, she submits to Mrs Creevy's regimen and suffers complete humiliation, but is finally restored to home and safety. At the same time, Dorothy in her role as teacher becomes a rather Lawrentian heroine. Despite the chapter's obvious literary sources, it is based on Orwell's personal experience and represents his most sustained discussion of the aims of education, of how children learn and how they should be taught.

Dorothy soon discovers that her pupils are almost completely ignorant, have learned the little they do know by rote, and cannot ask nor answer questions. She pities their apathy and ignorance, buys books and materials, divides them into groups according to age and ability, and teaches them individually. She believes in 'making, rather than learning' and, rather than drilling them in facts they do not understand, guides the children to participate actively in learning. The children learn geography by constructing a three-dimensional map of the world, history by making a time-chart. Dorothy feels that 'no job is more fascinating than teaching if you have a free hand at it', and delights in the 'unlooked-for gleams of intelligence' in her pupils' eyes. But the villainous Mrs Creevy destroys her developing relationship with the children and forces her to accede to the 'dirty swindle' of 'practical education'.

Critics have noted the influence on Orwell of Dickens's crusading novels of education, especially *Nicholas Nickleby* (1839), written to attack the Yorkshire private boarding-schools. Mrs Creevy's name sounds like that of Mr Creakle, the vicious schoolmaster in *David Copperfield*, though it also suggests her 'creepy' manner of spying and pouncing on her victims. In this respect she most resembles Mrs Sparsit, the angular, obsessive, sinister watcher and housekeeper in *Hard Times* (1854). Mrs Creevy's emphasis on 'practical' knowledge recalls the views of Mr Gradgrind (the schoolmaster in *Hard Times*), who stresses facts and the importance of stamping out imagination. Dorothy's indignation is expressed in Victorian rhetoric, and perhaps represents a satiric comment on Orwell's own recent foray into school-teaching. She reflects, 'the poor children, the poor children! How they had been stunted and maltreated!' and resolves to educate herself so that she can 'rescue [them] from the horrible darkness in which they had been kept'.

The atmosphere of the school owes something, too, to Wells's Mr Polly, who is sent to a private school of 'dingy aspect and still dingier pretensions' where 'the studies of book-keeping and French were pursued (but never effectually overtaken) under the guidance of an elderly gentleman, who ... wrote copperplate [and] explained nothing' (*The History of Mr Polly*, ch. 1). Like Dickens and Wells, Orwell attacks the stultifying effects of this kind of education, and argues that teachers have a moral obligation to teach children to think.

Like a crusading journalist, Orwell argues that Dorothy's experience is typical of this type of school. Staffed by the incompetent and alcoholic, subject to the parents' whims, they are businesses dominated by greed in which both teachers and children are exploited. Just as *Burmese Days* exposes the hypocrisy of British colonial rule, so this novel attacks the sham of the private school. Dorothy's relation to the children is parallel to Flory's to the Burmese. In order to obey Mrs Creevy, she resorts to bullying and betrays the children's trust; in order to win Elizabeth, Flory subscribes to hypocrisy and betrays Veraswamy.

Though the setting and atmosphere of this section of the novel owe much to Dickens and Wells, Orwell's account of Dorothy's struggle with her class and Mrs Creevy is closer to D. H. Lawrence's *The Rainbow*, suppressed on first publication in 1915, but reprinted in 1926. Chapter 13 of this novel describes Ursula Brangwen's humiliating first experience as a teacher, with an uncontrollable class and a brutal headmaster, Mr Harby. At first Ursula dreams that she will make the children love her, but she soon learns that current teaching methods are an 'evil system where she must brutalise herself to live'. She beats the boys into submission, dominates the class and succeeds as a teacher, but at the price of her own self-esteem. Like Ursula, Dorothy is forced to follow a soul-destroying, mechanical formula.

CONCLUSION: THE CONFLICT OF FORM AND MEANING

By chapter 4 Dorothy has become so much a vehicle for Orwell's ideas about teaching that her sudden removal from the school forces an abrupt transition to the original narrative frame. Once more she is rescued, and once more rebuffs Warburton's advances. Warburton is a means of returning her to Knype Hill and he interprets her story. He explains that Dorothy's loss of memory was caused by the unbearable conflict in her life. Dorothy is thus made to discuss her changed attitudes. While at Ringwood Dorothy had seen her loss of faith as simply 'a change in the climate of the mind'. Now she recognises that 'faith vanishes, but the need for faith remains the same', that 'though her faith had left her, she ... did not want to change the spiritual background of her mind'. The Christian life still has the traditional 'comeliness' she admires, and she sees no reason to repudiate it. Paradoxically, she realises (like the agnostic Victorians) that when you have no formal religious belief you have a greater need to construct a personal morality. The circularity of the plot and time-scheme emphasises Dorothy's acceptance of the life she had fled in the beginning.

This awkward conclusion underlines the basic contradiction,

running through the book, between the narrator's indignant drive to change society and the protagonist's acceptance of things as they are. Dorothy's extraordinary experiences have not changed her. Orwell recognised this conflict in himself in 'Why I Write', when he said that, however much he desired social change, he had no wish to change the world-view he had grown up with. In more general terms, Dorothy's story enacts Orwell's attempt to escape from his background, and his realisation that, for the moment at least, he could not.

Orwell fails to blend the various kinds of narrative in the novel chiefly because he lacks control over the narrative point of view. The conflict between narrator and heroine is particularly obvious in his treatment of women in the novel. Orwell's other works have many sympathetic references to women: in *Wigan Pier* and 'Wigan Pier Diary' he shows understanding and respect for women's courage and hard work; in *Keep the Aspidistra Flying* he created a loving heroine, in *Nineteen Eighty-Four* a spirited one. But in this novel his sympathetic portrait of Dorothy contrasts with the narrator's frequent disparagement of women.

Nagging, spying female characters surround her: Mrs Semprill, Mrs Creevy and Mrs Welwyn-Foster, the Rural Dean's wife, who gossips to the Bishop. Dorothy wakes, in chapter 1, to the alarm-clock's 'nagging, feminine clamour'. Orwell's reference to the cups of tea Dorothy is offered (an ironic echo of Walt Whitman's 'Out of the Cradle Endlessly Rocking': 'out of the teapot endlessly stewing') emphasises the limited lives of women. Just after Mrs Semprill first appears, Orwell refers to 'the day, like some overripe but hopeful widow'. Warburton assumes, in his long lecture in the last chapter, that marriage is the only possible life for a woman, and that a woman without a man will simply 'wither up like aspidistras in back-parlour windows'. Orwell seems particularly hostile to the widowed Mrs Semprill and Mrs Creevy, who are stereotyped witches rather than characters in a modern novel. These gratuitous references and caricatured portraits are at odds with the central character, who wants a life without marriage, dreads nagging her father and avoids gossip.

Orwell seems to forget that the story should be told from Dorothy's angle of vision. In chapter 4, for example, her direct explanation of 'womb' in *Macbeth*, which gets her into so much trouble, is quite out of keeping with her neurotic fear of sex. Her inner observation, during the painful interview with the parents, of the 'colourless, peculiarly *flat* wife who looked as though she had been flattened out by the pressure of some heavy object – her husband perhaps' belongs to the sophisticated male narrator, rather than the nervous and insecure young woman. In theory, Orwell uses Dorothy's experience to explore his ideas about English society and his own place it it. In practice, Dorothy is neither the fully developed character of realistic fiction (in spite of Orwell's attempts to inject some psychological explanation of her behaviour), nor the representative type that a didactic novel requires.

In *A Clergyman's Daughter* Orwell explored several ideas: the loss of faith, the precariousness of identity, the connection of identity with money, the necessity for compromise to survive in a society where one man's comfort depends on another's misery, the value of history and the sense of connection to the past. The novel vividly sketches the economically depressed, stagnant, class-bound England of the 1930s. But it is less successful in blending diverse genres. The fresh documentary detail of chapters 2 and 3 and the essay-like argument of chapter 4 show up the derivative fictional styles of the rest of the novel. Orwell's essential problem was the difficulty of adapting the traditional novel form, which depicts personal relationships in a settled society, to his true purpose, which was to analyse the social structure and argue for political change.

5

Keep the Aspidistra Flying:
Orwell's Portrait of the Artist

> ... whatever costs you money, money, money,
>   is really no fun.
> That's why women aren't much fun. You're always
>   having to pay for them.
>
> D. H. Lawrence, 'Always this paying', *Pansies*

Orwell hastily wrote *Keep the Aspidistra Flying* in 1935, in the hope of making some money, while he was living in Hampstead and working in a bookshop in South End Green. Though the character of Gordon Comstock is by no means identical with Orwell the man, his situation is closely modelled on Orwell's life at the time. The incidents and characters described in the novel are sufficiently close to real life for friends to have identified themselves in it. One of his girlfriends, Kay Ekevall, remembered Orwell's obsession with money, his old-fashioned insistence on paying for outings and dislike of 'going dutch', and a specific occasion when Orwell spent all his money on a dinner for a group of friends, got drunk and assaulted a policeman.[43] Ravelston, the editor of *Antichrist*, is a mildly satirical portrait of his friend Sir Richard Rees, the editor (with John Middleton Murry) of the *Adelphi*, a magazine where Orwell published many early essays and poems. Indeed, as Keith Alldritt has pointed out, Gordon's poem in chapter 7 of the novel was published by Orwell in the *Adelphi* in November 1935. 'Willowbed Road' and 'Coleridge Grove' suggest the nearby Willoughby Road and Keats Grove. The Lorings resemble Orwell's Hampstead circle of literary friends. Gordon's affair with Rosemary, their country walks and eventual marriage parallel Orwell's courtship and marriage (in 1936) to Eileen O'Shaughnessy.

Like most of Orwell's protagonists, Gordon Comstock is physically and morally trapped. He has given up a secure job in an advertising agency for a poorly paid job in a bookshop, believing that by living cheaply and writing poetry he would be able to escape the compromises of everyday life. But, as the novel begins, he discovers that without money he can neither write nor live decently. Having rejected his family background, Gordon has lost his social identity and feels alienated from almost everyone. He does not have the money to be upper-class, the conformity to be middle-class, the resignation to be working-class. Full of self-pity and self-hatred, he magnifies his isolation and imagines snubs where none are intended. He has two unpalatable alternatives: if he goes on in his present way of life he will sink lower, and produce no poetry; if he marries he will become a wage-slave, with no time to write.

As in both his earlier novels Orwell has a firm grip on the economic and social background of the characters (Gordon and Rosemary's strained lunch in the pretentious Thameside restaurant, for example), the documentary details (exactly how much Gordon pays for his room, and what he gets to eat), and vivid minor characters (like the woman who smells of old breadcrusts and tries to sell Gordon some filthy old books). But Orwell's attempt to give dramatic shape to Gordon's dilemma is much less successful. The novel is organised around Gordon's inner debate about how he can get out of (or whether he should sink deeper into) his messy life. But Ravelston, his best friend, and Rosemary, his girlfriend, his only confidants, cannot understand his dilemma nor help him resolve it. In his discussions with them, and in his own thinking, Gordon circles negatively around the problem, and is never able to imagine any positive mode of action. His final decision, like Dorothy's return to Knype, is somewhat arbitrary and inconsistent.

The beginning of the novel follows the pattern of Orwell's earlier books: the first chapter introduces the central, isolated character in typical mood and setting; the next describes his daily life and gives some explanation of how and why he has arrived in his present situation. But *Keep the Aspidistra Flying* prolongs the focus on Gordon alone for a full four chapters. Ravelston does not appear until chapter 5, Rosemary not until chapter 6, nearly half-way through the novel. Orwell's detailed emphasis on Gordon's biography and state of mind not only delays the action but betrays an underlying purpose – to write an auto-biography to explain and justify himself. Because Gordon is prim-arily a vehicle for expressing Orwell's own self-doubt, guilt and anxiety about his decision to be a writer, the novel tends to be static, repetitive and inconclusive, the narrative awkwardly inconsistent. The novel's rather obvious, strident theme is the destructive power of money and the insecurity of modern man in mass civilisation. The more important, though less articulate, theme is the question of what kind of social and moral identity is possible for a writer.

THE NOVEL AS AUTOBIOGRAPHY

In the first chapter Orwell sketches Gordon's character, introduc-ing motifs – the empty cigarette packet, the few coins, especially the joey, or threepenny piece, in his pocket, the foul weather, the intrusive billboard with the rat-faced clerk advertising 'Bovex' – which establish the sardonic mood and recur throughout the novel. Gordon lounges in the shop, horribly bored, where books and customers alike disgust him. He is obsessed with lack of money; dread of what other people, particularly women, think of him; the seven thousand decaying books all around him; his own inability to write; and with the oppressive ugliness of modern civilisation.

In appearance at least Gordon is exactly the opposite of Orwell himself: frail, short, pale, mousy-haired, shabbily dressed, un-shaven and none too clean. Though he is from the same middle-class background, his experience of life is limited. He lacks any knowledge or insight into politics, or even interest in other people. But Gordon's vehement self-criticism, his passionate sensitivity to class distinctions, his shame about his family background, and his weakness of character reveal his similarities to Flory, Orwell's earlier anti-hero. Like Flory, Gordon is lonely and longs for a wife, yet resents and fears women; though fiercely idealistic, he can also be hypocritical. He asks the middle-class customer if she has enjoyed *The Forsyte Saga*, though he despises both her and Galsworthy. He is a social coward, intimidated by his land-lady as he makes an illegal cup of tea, or easily faced down by a waiter with a fake French accent. Gordon also reminds us of Flory when he remarks to Ravelston that there are but three choices open to him: socialism, the Catholic Church, or suicide. Since he despises the first two, the last would seem to be, as it was for Flory, the only way out of his dilemma.

If we compare the account of Gordon's family and education in chapter 3 with the autobiographical reflections in *The Road to Wigan Pier* and 'Such, Such Were the Joys', we can see that Orwell drew freely on his own experience, character and opinions to create Gordon. The attack on Gordon's name and all things 'Scotch' reflects Orwell's dislike of his family's pride in their Scottish name and ancestry. In 'Such, Such' he scorns the snobbish delight of boys at his prep school who boasted of holidays in Scotland. Gordon's family, who have descended from pre-war affluence to genteel poverty, is like Orwell's own, as described in *Wigan Pier*: the bottom layer of the upper middle class, 'a sort of mound of wreckage left behind when the tide of Victorian prosperity receded' (ch. 8). Comstock's father, who carried with him 'an atmosphere of failure, worry and boredom' (rather like Gordon himself), is based on Orwell's elderly, retired father, who had to maintain his family on a Colonial Service pension. The sacrifice of the daughter's education for the sake of 'the boy', who is then expected to retrieve the family fortunes, and the guilt of the child, who is deeply ashamed of his parents and resents them for exposing him to the 'snobbish agonies' of a smart school, were later described with greater complexity in 'Such, Such Were the Joys'.

In that essay Orwell relates in bitter detail how the school considered him 'an examination-passer' whose fate it was to 'grind upwards, a hanger-on of the people who really counted' (*CEJL*, 4.356). He notes how his classmates, the children of those who counted, assumed that they would always have charm, beauty and 'character', a quality that, Orwell divined, meant 'the power to impose your will on others'. Like Orwell, Gordon slacked off after getting his scholarship to public school and concentrated on his private reading and intellectual development, instead of trying to do well academically. He suffers from the same combination of envy, snobbery and guilt described in 'Such, Such'. Gordon envies the 'moneyed beasts' (like the 'Nancy' client in the bookshop who adores 'poetwy') because without effort they get everything he wants – comfort, leisure, culture.

Gordon's hatred of the upper classes paralyses him, preventing him from trying to advance economically or socially. He wants to sink into the 'sub-world' where there are no jobs, 'no hope, fear, ambition, honour, duty', just as Orwell, by his own account in *Wigan Pier*, wanted to find some way of getting out of the respectable world altogether', to 'touch bottom' so that 'part of my guilt would drop from me'. Gordon feels guilty for snobbishly rejecting his family and betraying their sacrifice for his education. His sister Julia's tearful pleas to Gordon to go back to a good job dramatises Orwell's family's uncomprehending response to his decision to give up his career in Burma.

In 'Such, Such', written some years after this novel, Orwell was able to define much more clearly the ambivalent emotions his prep-school teachers had aroused in him. On the one hand, he wanted to please them, to earn their praise and develop his abilities; on the other, he knew that he would never possess the 'charm' of being someone who 'counted', and he loathed and feared the thrill of exerting power over others. Like Flory, Gordon embodies Orwell's conflicting feelings about himself, which became acute when he made a break with his career and committed himself to be a professional writer. Orwell understood that being a writer means asserting one's importance, staking one's special claim to be heard, imposing 'one's will on others'. He wanted this, of course, but at the same time he felt a contrary urge, a desire to wallow in obscurity and shame. Gordon's extreme disgust at the Bovex poster makes sense in the light of Sambo's threat that if Orwell did not win his scholarship he would become 'a little office boy at forty pounds a year' (*CEJL*, 4.340). The rat-faced clerk was Orwell's boyhood nightmare.

The close biographical links between Orwell himself and Gordon suggest his chief problem in this novel: his inability to distinguish adequately between the narrator and the central character. For roughly half the book the harshly satirical narrative voice expresses virtually the same negative attitudes and ideas as Gordon does. The tone is serio-comic, as critical of Gordon's pretensions and self-delusions as he is of others. The account of Gordon's family background in chapter 3 is entirely from Gordon's point of view, as is the description of Doring's literary parties in chapter 4. The narrative distinguishes between Gordon's expectation of the parties and the disappointing reality of them, yet it is clear that Gordon shares the narrator's cynical view:

Doring was kind in a slapdash way and introduced him to

everybody as 'Gordon Comstock – *you* know; the poet. He wrote that dashed clever book of poems called *Mice. You* know.' But Gordon had never yet encountered anyone who *did* know. The bright young things summed him up at a glance and ignored him. He was thirtyish, moth-eaten, and obviously penniless. And yet, in spite of the inevitable disappointment, how he looked forward to those literary tea-parties! They were a break in his loneliness, anyway. That is the devilish thing about poverty, the ever-recurrent thing – loneliness.

In chapters 5, 6 and 7 we see Ravelston and Rosemary through Gordon's eyes. Though kind, Ravelston is too comfortably off to understand Gordon's bitterness. Rosemary's reluctance to have sex and her fear of pregnancy are seen from Gordon's disappointed perspective.

Orwell uses many ironic poetic allusions to characterise Gordon (in chapter 1 alone Gordon refers to Keats, Marvell, Kipling, Villon, Baudelaire and *Hamlet*). But, since the narrator employs the same habit, we identify the narrator with the main character. The opening sentences of chapter 3 suggest Gordon's thoughts: 'Gordon Comstock was a pretty bloody name....' But after a couple of sentences Orwell's essay style intrudes: 'The prevalence of such names nowadays is merely a part of the Scotchification of England that has been going on these last fifty years.' Gordon is Orwell's satirical self-portrait, his musings the diary of a nobody who wants to be a somebody in the literary world. A person of mediocre talents, selfish and prone to self-pity, he quotes Baudelaire and sees himself cursed with poetry, a sufferer for art. In practice he rarely writes anything. He could have been a comic character, but Orwell's depiction of Gordon's anger, frustration and difficulties as a writer are completely serious.

In chapter 8 the narrative stance shifts, as the narrator distances himself more and more from the central character. As Gordon becomes drunk and out of control, we see him from Ravelston and Rosemary's point of view. He seems both foolish and pathetic, especially when he refuses all help and descends 'underground' in chapter 10. The scene of sexual consummation is presented from Rosemary's viewpoint; she initiates it, out of magnanimity, and her feelings ('dismayed, disappointed, and very cold'), not Gordon's, are described. Just as Gordon's view of life changes by the end of the novel, so the narrator's attitude toward him changes. Gordon begins as an ex-middle-class angry young man, a mocking caricature of Orwell the would-be poet, and ends as a Wellsian 'little man', happy to accept a lowly place in the world in exchange for peace of mind. The changing tone, from satiric and serious to comic and affectionate, reveals Orwell's shifting attitude to his hero.

GORDON COMSTOCK, THE WRITER WITHOUT POLITICS

Gordon is a most Lawrentian character, who wants to find out how to live, how to be a writer in a useful and honourable way. He expresses, often in crude and exaggerated form, Orwell's confused and contradictory ideas about class, sex and the political system. Gordon's arguments with Rosemary about women and marriage and with Ravelston about politics are the real heart of the novel; and, at least until the final chapters, give it the air of still debating the issues, of not quite knowing what the answers are. Unfortunately these discussions do not resolve the issues which divide Gordon from his friends, nor do they produce a solution to his dilemma. Gordon vents his anger and frustration, but all his arguments are for inaction, withdrawal or destruction. Essentially Gordon asks whether he should stay 'inside the whale' of society, accepting its terms and writing within its norms, or whether he should, like the Romantic poet, be outside, aggressive, critical and subversive. Marriage to Rosemary would seem to draw him inside, adopting Ravelston's political views would put him outside, but neither position suits him.

Gordon condemns women as selfish and cold. In the first chapter a series of women, each representative of her class, enter the bookshop, each one stupid, limited, lacking in taste. Several women humiliate Gordon in the course of the novel: the shopgirl who sneers at him; Mrs Wisbeach, who spies on him and forbids female visitors; the tarts in Piccadilly who trap and rob him; the librarian who assumes he is 'another male in search of dirt' when, in the first flush of enthusiasm about being a father, he asks for a book on gynaecology; and Hermione, Ravelston's rich girlfriend, who treats him contemptuously. Hermione's selfishness is gratuitously assigned to her sex, rather than her class.

Completely insulated by wealth, she has no sympathy for the down-and-out man outside the restaurant, and actually prevents Ravelston from giving him some money. Hermione exhales 'a woman-scent', 'a powerful wordless propaganda against all altruism and all justice'.

Gordon ponders 'the woman-question' gloomily in his discussion with Ravelston in chapter 5 and on his solitary walk home in chapter 6. Though he is lonely, and longs for Rosemary's love, he believes that women merely use sex to secure a house, furniture and babies, that 'marriage is only a trap set for you by the money-god'. He continues this argument when he meets Rosemary in the market, trying to trick her into admitting that she will not sleep with him because he has no money, and asserting that women have 'a mystical feeling towards money'. But Rosemary's good-natured, common-sense response cancels out his anger. She dismisses Gordon's views as 'palpable nonsense', his diatribes as just part of the 'perverse joke' which is the sex-war, 'the eternal and idiotic question of Man versus Woman'.

Just as Ravelston is generous and sensitive, an exception to the class Gordon loathes, so Rosemary is the exception to Gordon's idea of women. She is kind, unselfish, patient and loving, and, although she does finally get a husband and a household, she never manipulates Gordon. When their love-making turns into an embarrassing fiasco she caresses him tenderly, 'because in her feminine way she grasped that he was unhappy and that life was difficult for him'.

Although poverty and unemployment are widespread, and the fear of losing one's job contaminates the atmosphere, Gordon has dropped out of the respectable world for fear of being one of the mass, 'the black herds of clerks scurrying underground like ants into a hole'. He imagines himself a poet, a Byronic individual in a mass civilisation. His attitude to contraception (which he calls 'filthy cold-blooded precautions') is irresponsible and selfish, but he regards it, like 'mind-rotting' advertising, as a sinister means of state control.

Ravelston believes in Marxist revolution, while Gordon is anti-everything and sees no possibility of change for the better. In their discussions, he tries to justify his inaction and negativity. He has flirted with Communism, but has seen through that 'stodgy bait'. Ravelston urges him to read Marx, so that he would see that Marx had predicted this collapse of the economy: the desperate poverty and unemployment of the period was just 'Capitalism in its last phase. I doubt whether it's worth worrying about.' Ravelston's point of view is clearly as 'inside the whale' as Rosemary's – he simply adheres to another set of conventions. His naïve belief in the ultimate success of the proletarian revolution allows him to enjoy his unearned income, avoid worrying about the unemployed, and feel morally right. Gordon's image of the socialist state, like his anti-feminist assertions, is also a provocative joke: model factories, mass-production, communal kitchens, free abortions. But Ravelston offers no common-sense rebuttal.

Gordon compares adherence to socialism with membership in the Roman Catholic Church, that 'standing temptation to the intelligentsia'. The temptation consisted in the view (of T. S. Eliot and other conservative thinkers) that, since industrialisation had spawned an uneducated mass society without religious belief, the intellectual's duty was to form a cultural and spiritual elite which would govern a traditional, hierarchical society. This would assure the writer, at least in theory, a privileged status. Gordon's contempt for the masses suggests that he would find the conservative, even Fascist, position appealing. Orwell believed Catholicism and Marxism had much in common, and he satirised both in *Animal Farm*; both offered a system of belief which stressed ultimate rewards – heaven, or a perfect state.

But the political issues are not really explored, let alone resolved, in the debates between Gordon and Ravelston. Gordon feels that Ravelston's own life and attitudes disqualify his arguments for socialism; Gordon will not even give him full credit for his decency and kindness, because 'money buys all virtues'. Their differences derive solely from money: with eight hundred pounds a year Ravelston can afford to be positive about the future; Gordon on two pounds a week feels he'd like to 'see our money-civilization blown to hell by bombs'. In the first chapter Gordon identifies his own physical decay with the 'sense of disintegration . . . endemic in our time'. He connects advertising (the promotion of mass-consumption) with the menace of coming war. The ubiquitous Bovex poster makes him think of 'French letters and machine-guns' – instruments of control and destruction. These discussions only lead back to his initial urges: to go 'underground' or to join the universal death-wish that is in the air.

THE LITERARY SOURCES OF ORWELL'S
PORTRAIT OF THE ARTIST

Despite its autobiographical parallels, Gordon's character was also influenced by earlier novels on similar themes, especially Joyce's *A Portrait of the Artist as a Young Man* (1916) and Wyndham Lewis's *Tarr* (1918). Lawrence's *Lady Chatterley's Lover* (1928) provided the novel with its resolution and its secondary theme of the condition of England.

Gordon's self-disgust and passivity derive from Joyce's Stephen Dedalus in *A Portrait of the Artist*.[44] Like Stephen, Gordon is hypersensitive to the squalor of his own body and surroundings, the contrast between his sordid physical life and his idealistic intellectual aspirations. Gordon's mind is similarly stocked with poetic allusions. Stephen feels cut off by poverty from the girl he admires, just as Gordon imagines the girls in the market shrinking from his glance, and assumes Rosemary will reject him. Once again Orwell draws on the 'nighttown' episode of *Ulysses*, where Stephen gets drunk and consorts with prostitutes. In chapter 8, as Gordon gets drunker, he compares the lights of Piccadilly to those of hell, and as he follows the prostitute up the staircase he adopts Joyce's hell-imagery and alludes to Virgil's journey to the underworld in the *Aeneid*. Orwell imitates Joyce's stream-of-consciousness technique in the rest of the chapter, as Gordon's scrambled thoughts show him becoming increasingly out of control.

Orwell was also greatly impressed by Joyce's challenging assertion of the key role of the artist in society. Stephen's declaration, at the end of *A Portrait of the Artist*, that he will 'go to encounter for the millionth time the reality of experience and forge in the smithy of my soul the uncreated conscience of my race' movingly expresses Joyce's idea that the artist shapes his nation's collective identity. Orwell certainly agreed that the writer's task was to confront reality and stir society's conscience. But Orwell's novel finally rejects Joyce's Romantic notion of the artist as somehow set apart from, superior to, ordinary people. Orwell ridicules Gordon's attempt to live the bohemian poet's life. There is no audience for Gordon's dog-eared *London Pleasures*. Dull in style and false in content (an ironic contrast to Gordon's *real* London), it is torture to write, and bores its creator to death. But Orwell evades the issue of whether or not the writer should consider himself a special person. He precludes a genuine argument by making Gordon an unexceptional person.

Gordon's perverse pleasure in losing his job and sinking even lower than before, his desire to be *underground* (ch. 10) has its antecedent in the hero of Dostoevsky's *Notes from Underground* (1864), who constantly courts and relishes humiliation. Orwell knew and admired Wyndham Lewis's *Tarr*, a novel of bohemian expatriate Paris strongly influenced by Dostoevsky. Lewis's Kreisler, a German painter, who combines the self-destructive hatred and violence of Dostoevsky's hero with the frustrated ambition of the failed artist, provides an ironic contrast to Tarr, the artist hero of the novel. Reclusive, yet craving attention, Kreisler makes a fool of himself at bourgeois soirées (just as Gordon feels ill-at-ease at the Dorings). Thirty-six years old, obsessed by 'class-inferiority-feeling', he has spent years studying art and is therefore unfit to earn his living. Creatively blocked and heavily in debt, he takes his own life. Some of Gordon's worst characteristics seem very close to Kreisler's: his stagnant creativity, his contempt for nearly everybody, his hatred of contemporary civilisation, his utter paralysis, his lack of money, and his intermittent desire to see the world destroyed. Lewis's impatience with the class system and the philistinism of the English ruling classes struck a responsive chord in Orwell. Gordon's scathing references to the well-dressed and well-connected 'moneyed beasts' and 'safe' poets and painters sound very like Lewis, in both his novels and essays.

Though Kreisler escapes his situation by committing suicide, many of Lewis's characters escape stultifying England by leaving. Lewis himself lived in France as a young man and later emigrated to Canada. Joyce and Lawrence both chose exile, and emigration is a recurring conclusion in Lawrence's novels and stories. For most of the novel, Orwell's hero shares this feeling that conditions in England itself prevent creativity. He thinks of his poems with 'contempt' and 'horror', as 'abortions', and tells Ravelston, echoing T. S. Eliot's *The Waste Land*, 'My poems are dead because I'm dead. You're dead. We're all dead. Dead people in a dead world.' Writing itself is a dead end, because it has no purpose.

Orwell adapts several elements of Lawrence's last novel, *Lady Chatterley's Lover*, in *Keep the Aspidistra Flying*. Gordon, like Mellors, has dropped out of the ordinary working world and is rescued from loneliness by a love affair; just as Mellors kisses

Connie's belly at the end of *Lady Chatterley*, so Gordon presses his head against Rosemary and imagines the baby growing inside her. Orwell's lovers resemble Lawrence's in significant ways: both couples are no longer young; they make love in the country-side, and find the city ugly and depressing; Rosemary is aware of Gordon's poverty and is careful to protect his dignity, just as the aristocratic Constance Chatterley defers to the hypersensit-ive, lower-class Mellors.

Gordon's distaste for contraception coincides with Lawrence's, though for different reasons. In *Lady Chatterley* Lawrence criticises the casual, meaningless sexual games of the leisured upper classes, made possible by contraception and abortion. Because Gordon associates the working-class with spontaneity, directness and naturalness, the middle-class with sexual coldness (as in Rosemary, who has inherited her family's outlook), he associates contraception with the deadly restraint of his background. Gordon naïvely salutes 'the factory lad who with fourpence in the world puts his girl in the family way! At least he's got blood in his veins!' Rosemary's pregnancy defies the Comstock 'money-code' and, like Connie's, represents hope for the future. But in Orwell the pregnancy represents compromise with social norms, in Lawrence defiance of them.

Orwell's use of Lawrence's key themes and techniques also shows up in the novel's vocabulary and imagery. Clifford Chatter-ley's worship of the 'bitch-goddess', success, is echoed in Gordon's frequent diatribes against the 'money-god'. Gordon's constant repetition of 'beastly', a key word in Lawrence's collec-tion of poems *Pansies*, also betrays the Lawrentian source. Gordon loathes and ill-treats the aspidistra in his room, a rather too-obvious symbol of gloomy respectability, but at the end of the novel it puts out green shoots and becomes a 'tree of life' – a serious Lawrentian image becoming a grim Orwellian joke. The novel's mocking title mimics the chorus of the revolutionary song 'The Red Flag': 'We'll keep the red flag flying high', and thus suggests the novel's foregone conclusion – that Gordon will not create a new way of life. In fact, ordinary English life will go on pretty much as it always has.

In chapter 11 of *Lady Chatterley*, Connie's view of Derbyshire towns and villages reflects her own sense of sterility and expresses the theme of the decay of England, the ugliness of the modern industrial landscape which blots out the past. Orwell uses the same theme and the method of relating the inner state of the central character to his surroundings. In chapter 1 Gordon gazes out of the bookshop at the leaden sky, windy street and torn advertisements, feels civilisation is dying and notes his own 'greyish reflection' in the window-pane. Gordon is obsessed with the idea which occurs frequently in Lawrence's work in the 1920s: that civilisation will be destroyed by another war soon to come, and that perhaps it deserves to be.

The problem, of course, with Orwell's use of these literary models is that the vehement feelings of Stephen, Kreisler or Mellors do not fit Gordon Comstock, and his actions do not match the extremity of his expression. Orwell ties up the ends of the story neatly, making Gordon recant his earlier wish to blow everything sky-high. But the real issue of the novel, the question of the writer's role in such a world, is not resolved. Gordon's disgust with books in general and his own in particular suggests Orwell's frustration with writing this very novel; perhaps he sat, like his hero, 'in a corner, torturing a nerve'. Clearly the traditional form could not sustain all his conflicting purposes. This was to be his last novel for several years, and the last to be so heavily derivative. In the years before his next novel, *Coming Up for Air*, Orwell explored his anxieties about England's future and his own in autobiography and non-fiction.

6

Coming Up for Air: Documentary into Novel

To have been born into a world of beauty, to die amid ugliness, is the common fate of all us exiles [from the pre-1914 era].

Evelyn Waugh, *A Little Learning*

In May 1937 Orwell was wounded in the Spanish Civil War, and early in 1938 he became for the first time seriously ill with tuberculosis. He wrote his fourth novel, *Coming Up for Air*, in Marrakech, Morocco, where he spent the winter of 1938–39 to recuperate. After *Keep the Aspidistra Flying*, Orwell's life and work changed decisively. He married in July 1936 and went to live in a village in Hertfordshire. *The Road to Wigan Pier*, his report on the conditions of unemployed workers, published by the Left Book Club early in 1937, made him known to a wider audience, and his experiences in the north of England and Spain confirmed his growing socialist convictions. His next book, *Homage to Catalonia*, an account of his experiences in the Spanish war, was a personal narrative, like *Wigan Pier*, which combined documentary observation, social and political commentary and autobiographical reflection.

In his essays, from the episodic 'Clink' (1932) and 'Hop Picking' (1931) to the more artfully shaped 'A Hanging' (1931) and 'Shooting an Elephant' (1936), Orwell had developed a distinctive documentary style, in contrast to the often weak and inconsistent technique of his early novels. In the essays his narrative 'I' not only describes events and settings in a concrete, analytic way, but also puts himself into the scene, and relates his response to the situation. The speaking 'I' unifies the material and articulates a moral vision of the subject, rather than merely describing it. Wigan and Spain were challenging subjects which aroused

Orwell's passions and led him to develop his essay style in full-length books.

The experience of writing these documentaries, and the success of *Wigan Pier*, affected *Coming Up for Air* in three important ways. First, the lengthy autobiographical section of *Wigan Pier* seems to have satisfied Orwell's need to define his identity and probe his guilt. Although a large part of the novel is autobiographical in form, autobiography is not its primary focus. Bowling's account emphasises childhood memories and is part of the novel's larger argument – the contrast of past and present. Secondly, the non-fiction books describe situations which demanded a consistent political viewpoint, where the muddled contradictions of Gordon Comstock were not possible. *Coming Up for Air* consequently has a clearer political focus. Finally, Orwell successfully adapted many features of his essay style to the novel. In the non-fiction he had developed a first-person reporting style, capable of travelling back and forth between private concerns and public issues, expressed in a vivid, colloquial language which placed abstract ideologies or economics in a compelling human context. In *Coming Up for Air* Orwell gives this effective narrative voice to the central character, George Bowling, whose thoughts flow confidently from his false teeth to unemployment or the coming war.

In a letter of 1948, Orwell responded to Julian Symons's criticism that Orwell's own character constantly intrudes on that of the narrator. 'I am not a real novelist anyway', Orwell wrote (*CEJL*, 4.422), asserting that this was the danger of writing a novel in the first person, 'which one should never do'. In spite of his admiration for modernist writers such as James Joyce and Henry Miller, Orwell had a rather narrow idea of what a novel should be. His chief model was Wells, and there are many Wellsian elements in *Coming Up for Air*: the lower-middle-class 'average man' hero who goes on a journey of escape from a stifling milieu (like Mr Polly); the narrator–protagonist's anger at the despoliation of natural landscape by urban development (*In the Days of the Comet*); the idea that a sleepy, decaying England of complacent small towns will be rudely awakened by destructive weapons of the future (*Tono-Bungay*). Wells's Mr Britling (in *Mr Britling Sees It Through*) is also a model for Bowling. While others seem 'asleep' he is aware of the danger of war (in this case the Great War) and the possibility of defeat. But *Coming Up for Air* is not at all Wellsian in form. Orwell's judgement to the contrary, the first-person narrative method works well here: it came most naturally to him, for it was the characteristic mode of the essays and documentaries; George Bowling is a far more consistent mouthpiece for Orwell's views than any other of his previous characters, and his point of view unifies the novel's themes and concentrates its message.

Orwell's autobiographical strain thus gives way to the political–polemical. This is a didactic novel, like *Animal Farm* and *Nineteen Eighty-Four*, written as a specific comment on the current political situation. The novel has two related themes: it is a lament for the destruction of pastoral Edwardian England and a complaint against the ugly machine-civilisation which has replaced it; and a warning of the approaching war, its destructive modern weaponry, and the danger of a Fascist takeover in Great Britain. It does not propose a political programme, but tries to capture the menacing mood of 1938, to articulate fears, and to reinforce the social values that Orwell felt were threatened by the coming war. When he was working on the book in Morocco in December 1938, Orwell described his mood in a letter to Cyril Connolly. He felt his work was 'overshadowed by this ghastly feeling that we are rushing towards a precipice' and that 'we ... must put up some sort of fight' (*CEJL*, 1.362). In 'Why I Write' (1946), Orwell dated his political commitment from 1936 and the Spanish war. Since that time everything he had written was '*against* totalitarianism and *for* democratic Socialism' (*CEJL*, 1.5). The form and content of Orwell's fiction are now shaped by his political purpose, and the novels become part of an ideological argument.

GEORGE BOWLING: CHARACTER AS STEREOTYPE

Coming Up for Air has the barest of plots: George Bowling, 'a fat middle-aged bloke with false teeth and a red face' (Part Two, ch. 1), a lower-middle-class insurance agent, decides to escape his family and spend his unexpected winnings from gambling on a week's holiday. He visits Lower Binfield, the Thames Valley market town where he grew up, in hopes of finding some echo of his past; he returns, somewhat disillusioned, to his suburban home and shrewish wife. Since Bowling's reflections on the past, his views of the present and anxiety about the future make up the entire novel, Orwell needed to create a plausible speaker, who represents the average man, yet is independent enough to think critically about the world around him.

As a basis for his character, Orwell borrowed the Wellsian device of using a mediocre protagonist to comment on social ills. Bowling not only physically resembles Wells's Mr Polly, who is 'thirty-seven, and fattish in a not very healthy way', but also shares Mr Polly's background as an Edwardian grocer's assistant.[45] Bowling claims this novel was one of the first serious books he had read, and suggests that he identified with the hero (Part Two, ch. 8). Bowling's entertaining narrative also suggests that Orwell was imitating Joyce's Bloom, the average sensual man of *Ulysses*, whose stream of consciousness takes up most of that novel. Orwell skilfully uses colloquialisms, slang and clichés ('scared stiff', 'several quid', 'her main kick in life') to suggest the speaking voice of a vulgar salesman with a practised patter.

As in his other novels, Orwell begins by presenting his central character at the start of a typical day, and carefully places him on the economic and class scale. Orwell went to some trouble to make Bowling credible. He wrote from Morocco to a friend who was an insurance agent, asking detailed questions about an agent's job and circumstances (*CEJL*, 1.358). Bowling is a 'five-to-ten-pound-a-weeker' who lives in a dreary outer suburb and rides the train to the head office in London. Bowling presents himself and his wife Hilda as stereotypes, people who are the sum of a list of sociological attributes, rather than individuals. Depressed and overweight, he wears 'the uniform of the tribe', and lives in one of a row of identical little stucco boxes with its worn patch of grass in front, mortgaged, like all the others, to the Cheerful Credit Building Society. Bowling sees himself as trapped into work to support his average two-child family.

In constructing these deliberately stereotypical characters, Orwell had in mind the conventions of the vulgar comic postcard, a genre he analysed in his essay 'The Art of Donald McGill' (1941). In this essay Orwell derived a list of common assumptions about life to be found in these examples of low English humour: all women seek and plot marriage, while men plot seduction; married couples are either young, attractive honeymooners, obsessed with love-making, or warring and middle-aged; the wives of the latter are shrivelled and shrewish, or fierce and bloated, husbands fat and red-nosed; all marriages are miserable after the honeymoon; and all women defeat men in argument. Bowling and Hilda fit these conventions perfectly. Hilda, once a 'pretty, delicate girl', gives up trying to please her husband as soon as she has secured him, and is now an ugly, joyless, nagging housewife afraid of having more children and obsessed with saving money. Bowling, conventionally misogynistic, escapes to the pub and womanises whenever he gets the chance. Hilda catches him out, of course.

In his essay Orwell relates the vulgar humour of these mis-shapen postcard characters to the profound and serious split in Western man, the 'ancient dualism of body and soul' represented by the fat Sancho Panza and the lean Don Quixote, in the novel by Cervantes. The one stands for earthy realism, the base common sense that saves its own skin first, the other the saintly, heroic ideal. Orwell made Bowling a stereotypical fat man to underline his role as spokesman for the 'unofficial self' inside the reader, 'the voice of the belly protesting against the soul' (*CEJL*, 2.163). Orwell liked to see the postcards hanging in the dusty racks at newsagents because, he wrote, 'whatever is funny is subversive'. Bowling mocks all the swindles of modern sub-urban life, from the 'neutral fruit-juice' in the breakfast jam, the illusory pride of 'home-ownership', Hilda's food-fads and spiritualism, to the propaganda of the Left Book Club lecturer.

Though outwardly a stereotype, Bowling has a critical perspective on his everyday life, gained chiefly from his strong attachment to the past. Inside this fat man of the present the thin man of the past is trying to get out. He asserts that, vulgar and insensitive as he is on the outside, inside he suffers from 'a hangover from the past' (Part One, ch. 3). Orwell gives us an autobiographical explanation for Bowling's unlikely sophistication. In his letter to his insurance agent friend Orwell had remarked that he wanted his protagonist to be, though plausibly typical, 'fairly well-educated, even slightly bookish'. Bowling has a long period of lonely reading and reflection on the north Cornish coast during the Great War, just as Orwell had in Burma. Just as Orwell's recent experience in the Spanish Civil War had clarified his political thinking, so the war itself has shattered Bowling's pre-1914 view of the world, for after 'that unspeakable idiotic mess you couldn't go on regarding society as something eternal and unquestionable .... You knew it was just a balls-up' (Part Two, ch. 8).

In the first chapter, when he tells his anecdote about the girl assistant humiliated by the store manager, Bowling observes, 'Fear! We swim in it.' This central metaphor of the novel, of coming up for air while swimming, or drowning, in the horrors of modern life, also serves to persuade us that Bowling is an 'average man', because it represents a temporary escape from work and family. His narrative is an occasion to articulate ideas which have no place in the narrator's normal life. As soon as Bowling returns from his foray into the past Hilda puts him back in his place. In the saloon-bar someone teases him about his weight by alluding to 'the hulk' of 'Tom Bowling', a traditional song which laments the death of a sailor, who goes aloft once more, to heaven (Part One, ch. 3).[46] The allusion suggests that George Bowling, the common man, may be submerged in the anonymity of his class and type, and as afraid as everyone else, but he *is* capable of coming up for air, rising up and refusing to accept the ugliness of his environment or the cruelty and waste of the war to come.

BOWLING'S JOURNEY: STRUCTURE AND THEME

Samuel Hynes has described *Coming Up for Air* as a 'visionary novel ... disguised as flat colloquial realism'.[47] Orwell creates the illusion that we are listening to Bowling's rambling mixture of nostalgic reminiscence and reflections on modern life, while the novel builds a prophetic political argument. On one level the novel is a fictional autobiography, a narrative which weaves back and forth in time in order to understand the present and anticipate the future; on another it is a polemical argument which employs the rhetorical device of contrast. The Great War, the crucial event which has changed English life, is Bowling's mental dividing line. He thinks constantly of 'then' and 'now', past and present: before 1914, life as he remembers it was pastoral, tranquil; now it is ugly, industrialised and menacing. The past was an idyll; the present is a nightmare. The novel puts Orwell's view of the state of England and the shape of things to come.

Though Bowling's recollections seem random and disconnected, they are carefully anchored to specific dates and places. In the opening chapter Bowling tells us that he is forty-five, and in the newspaper he notices a mention of the wedding of King

Zog (the Muslim king of Albania), which dates the novel's present as January 1938. In Part One, Bowling describes his present life and his 'prophetic mood', and the train of association set up by King Zog's name sends him back, in memory, to a Sunday morning in 1900, in the market-place in Lower Binfield, when he could breathe 'real air'; Part Two describes Bowling's childhood and his wartime experience, and ends by reminding us that 'now it's '38'. Part Three returns us to the evening of the same day as the opening chapter, describes the Left Book Club meeting, the visit to Porteous where they discuss Bowling's thoughts about Hitler and the war, which Bowling says will begin in 1941; the narrative jumps to March, when Bowling decides he will go to Lower Binfield, and then to June, when he actually goes. Part Four describes his visit there and ends with his return home. Places, as well as time, are very specifically described: in the present, Bowling's own house in Ellesmere Road, and the pub and tea shop in modern Binfield; in the past, his father's shop, the banks of the Thames and the carp pool behind Binfield House.

In Part Two, Bowling's present awareness of impending war and destruction is contrasted with successive images of past security and stability. Bowling's chief childhood memory is of summer, when he trespassed in secluded places and fished in solitude. He remembers evocative smells: the wild mint by the river-bank, the sacks of grain in his father's shop; and the small things important to a child: the variety of sweets available for a penny, such as Paradise Mixture, liquorice pistols, and prize packets; the kind of flies ('gentles' and greenbottles) or grubs (got with difficulty from wasps' nests) to use as bait; the 'bliss' of reading boys' penny weeklies, like the *BOP* (*Boys' Own Paper*) and *Chums*. The satisfying adventure plots and all-powerful heroes of his boyhood reading implicitly contrast with the real violence of the modern world and Bowling's present sense of bewilderment and powerlessness.

With adult hindsight Bowling draws contrasts between the simple wholesomeness of the past, rural economy, and the destructive effects of modern technology, centred in the cities and towns. He remembers the horse with his nosebag at the trough in the market square and contrasts it with the 'petrol stink' of cars. (Though many people would find the smell of horsedung just as offensive as petrol, Bowling assumes that because it is a natural odour it is therefore better.) Orwell asserts that, in spite of its power to create new possibilities, technology has destroyed variety and brought about a uniform drabness. Even the family dog, Nailer, was 'an old white English terrier of the breed that's gone out nowadays' (Part Two, ch. 1).

Bowling's father sells grain, the most basic and wholesome food. Of limited intelligence and modest ambition, he stands for the simple honesty possible in the stable period before the war. His claim to fame is, appropriately enough, a birdseed mixture known for five miles around, good for maintaining the kinds of caged birds which people no longer keep. Like Bowling's father, his mother is defined by her work, rolling pastry in her kitchen, confined to her household, indifferent to and ignorant of the outside world. Mrs Bowling's traditional English cooking ('the smell of roast pork and greens') contrasts sharply with the American-style fast-food bar in chapter 4 of Part One, where everything 'comes out of a carton or a tin, or it's hauled out of a refrigerator or squirted out of a tap or squeezed out of a tube'. Just as the young George reads about dauntless heroes who find treasure in exotic places, so his parents read the Sunday papers for old-fashioned murders and remote scandals and disasters. In 1900 Queen Victoria still reigns; in this world nothing threatens the unalterable peace.

The stability of society is reflected in the landscape itself. Bowling remembers that 'On top of the hills there were woods in sort of dim blue masses among which you could see a great white house with a colonnade' (Part Two, ch. 1). Binfield House suggests spaciousness, order and serenity. Though life was harsh for most in those days, and 'people ... worked harder, lived less comfortably, and died more painfully, they didn't think of the future as something to be terrified of' (Part Two, ch. 7). As Orwell remarked in a review of Osbert Sitwell's *Great Morning*, before 1914 'people had the inestimable advantage of not knowing that war was coming, or, if they did know it, of not foreseeing what it would be like' (*CEJL*, 4.445). Orwell's personal experience in Spain and the evidence of German brutality in the Condor Legion bombing of Guernica (a preview of the way civilian populations were attacked by bomber planes in the Second World War) gave him insight into the war to come.

But Orwell also shows the dark side of this golden world. In spite of its apparent security, Lower Binfield is already changing, even in Bowling's boyhood. Even before the war, the owner of Binfield House had found it too expensive to live in and abandoned it. It had been built when people 'imagined that the good days would last forever' (Part Two, ch. 4). Business declines and young George has to leave school early to get a job. The war accelerates change, and the Bowlings slide towards bankruptcy as small shops are replaced by big stores. Bowling thinks of Wordsworth's poetry of childhood when he describes the happiness of small boys fishing in an unspoiled countryside, but he also recalls their delight in stamping on chicks. 'Killing things', he says, '– that's about as near to poetry as a boy gets' (Part Two, ch. 4). In a particularly grisly observation, Orwell notes that the butcher's backyard, though excellent for collecting bait, 'smelt like a battlefield', an image which suggests both the decaying period and the carnage of the two wars to come. Bowling remembers his eleven-hour-a-day job as a grocery clerk, his practised servility, his paltry ambition to set up his own identical business. He sketches the cruel determinism of class in the anecdote about Katie, a girl from a poor and brutish family, who beomes pregnant at fifteen, a 'hag' at twenty-seven; the memory of his first love affair, with Elsie, is soiled by guilt, for he knows that he took advantage of the sexual hypocrisy and inequality of the period. When he sees her in present-day Binfield her startling physical decay seems to obliterate his pleasant memories of the past.

Nevertheless, Bowling's idyllic re-creation of the past provides a peaceful contrast to the novel's dominant mood and theme, the menace of war and the destructiveness of modern development. In Part One, Bowling relates the current of fear ('we swim in it') to the high unemployment and economic insecurity of the 1930s. Haunted by a sense of vulnerability and doom, both of the exterior world and the democratic system itself, he is in a 'prophetic mood', 'the only person awake in a city of sleepwalkers' (Part One, ch. 4). He has a frightening vision of an artificial future, in which technology plays a diabolical role:

> Celluloid, rubber, chromium-steel everywhere, arc-lamps blazing all night, glass roofs over your head, radios all playing the same tune, no vegetation left, everything cemented over, mock-turtles grazing under the neutral fruit trees.

He observes the roof-tops of London from a train-window, and imagines machine-guns firing from bedroom windows (some-thing Orwell had seen in Spain two years before). In Part Four bombers fly over Binfield, and Bowling sees children parading in gas-masks. 'Already we're listening for the first bomb', he says, and the novel ends shortly after the accidental fall of 'one of ours' in the main street, which kills three people.

In Part Three, Bowling's apocalyptic mood intensifies when he attends the Left Book Club meeting, where the ranting lecturer builds a readiness for war by making the Germans a focus of hate (which prefigures the 'two minutes' hate' in *Nineteen Eighty-Four*). Eager to share his anxiety, Bowling goes to visit his friend Porteous, a retired shoolmaster, whose resigned attitude contrasts with Bowling's sense of urgency. Like Mr Hare in *A Clergyman's Daughter*, Porteous is a satiric stereotype who shuts out the modern world, and represents the false but seductive security of living among books, in a 'masculine' environment that pre-cludes all conflict. Believing Hitler ephemeral, Porteous refuses to be concerned and retreats into poetry, while Bowling feels the world collapsing about him.

Ironically, of course, Porteous does what Bowling is tempted to do – stop worrying about the future and retreat into the golden memory of the past. But Bowling rejects this, and urges the reader to reject it too. Just as Gordon Comstock realises that his poems are lifeless because he and everyone else are living in the past, so Bowling concludes that intellectuals like Porteous are virtually dead beause their 'minds have stopped'. Porteous's decision to ignore the modern world means passive acceptance of anything that happens. In the twenty years since the last war, Bowling asserts, the 'vital juice' has gone out of us, so that we are simply waiting for the 'bad time' ahead. Porteous is an exaggerated version of the prevailing passive attitude, even among educated people, which Orwell wanted to change.

The fishing motif, picked up again and again in the novel, in Part Four completes Orwell's lament for a lost way of life. In Bowling's boyhood fishing is a peaceful, reflective refuge; in his adolesence he is offered the chance to fish the huge carp in the secluded pool behind Binfield House, but he goes there only once. Just before the war he goes there again with Elsie (who is also named Waters, like the salesman in the bar), but makes love to her instead of exploring the pool. As a soldier during the war in France he goes to great lengths to sneak off to go fishing, but is sent into action instead, wounded, and then sent to north Cornwall. His next thought of fishing does not occur until years later, when he is on holiday at Bournemouth with Hilda and the kids, and Hilda sharply forbids it. But because the pool at Binfield House remains a cherished memory, when he sets off on his illicit journey he imagines he is actually going back to the past.

His disillusionment with unrecognisable modern Binfield, its surroundings 'buried by a kind of volcanic eruption from the outer suburbs', culminates in his visit to the Thames and to Binfield House. Bowling buys the rod and tackle he has coveted for years, only to discover the once-empty river-meadows loud with popular music and crowded with people, teahouses and ice-cream stalls. His mental image of silently, peacefully fishing alone gives way to a grotesque 'continuous chain of men fishing, one every five yards', in oily, littered water. When he finally gets to Binfield House (now a 'loony bin' – symbolic of those remnants of the gentry still in positions of power) he finds the land deforested and turned into a pretentious housing estate with hideous fake Tudor architecture. Orwell's final image of a despoiled England is the lovely, secret pool, now drained and turned into a rubbish dump, already half-full of tin cans.

THE NOVEL AS ARGUMENT

The colloquial first-person narrative allowed Orwell to include in the novel the various kinds of essays he was particularly good at: the evocative autobiography (the sections on Bowling's fishing, his reading, his time in the army); the observations of popular culture (sweet-shops, the decor of pubs and teashops, Hilda's meetings and fads); and the political opinion essay. The rambling, associative form permits Orwell to express ideas about many topics related to his theme of the decay of the modern world: unemployment, mechanisation, suburbs, mortgages, domestic architecture, synthetic food.

Instead of the scene-setting and character description of the conventional novel, Orwell uses the techniques of argument to project the narrator's point of view. As we have seen, the basic structure of the novel rests on Bowling's contrast between 'then' and 'now', the idyll of the past showing up the horrors of the

present and future. Bowling's discussion with Porteous in Part
Three, rather like Gordon's with Ravelston and Rosemary in
Keep the Aspidistra Flying, clarifies his position and forestalls
opposition, just as one might attack a counter-argument in
debate.

Orwell also uses Bowling to appeal to the reader's aesthetic
and moral senses. He creates lists of repellent images or objects,
taken from contemporary news reports. In a key passage Bowling
predicts a totalitarian nightmare:

> The coloured shirts, the barbed wire, the rubber truncheons.
> The secret cells where the electric light burns night and day,
> and the detectives watching you while you sleep. And the pro-
> cessions and the posters with enormous faces . . . . It's all going
> to happen.   (Part Three, ch. 1)

This passage suggests prison cells and concentration camps,
Stalin's purge trials and Hitler's Nuremberg rallies. In his essay
on 1930s literature, 'Inside the Whale', making a similar point
to Bowling's, Orwell argues that the writer should not accept
the world as it is, but use his work to protest:

> To say 'I accept' in an age like our own is to say that you
> accept concentration camps, rubber truncheons, Hitler, Stalin,
> bombs, aeroplanes, tinned food, machine-guns, putsches,
> purges, slogans, Bedaux belts, gas-masks, submarines, spies,
> *provocateurs*, press censorship, secret prisons, aspirins, Holly-
> wood films and political murders.   (*CEJL*, 1.499–500)

Orwell wittily juxtaposes images of war, death and political terror
with modern objects he detests – tinned food, aspirin and Holly-
wood films. Though these seem innocuous enough, they represent
manifestations of the machine: adulterated, tasteless food, chemi-
cal palliatives, and false, sentimental, propagandistic popular
art.

As Orwell does in *Wigan Pier*, Bowling frequently argues from
anecdote. Early in the novel he tells the story about the shop-
assistant and concludes from it that all men live in fear of unemployment. Or he argues from a single sensory example, such
as the fishy-tasting sausage which bursts in his mouth (as the
bomb explodes at the end of the novel), which represents the

degradation of basic English food in favour of the ersatz or Americanised fast food. In *Wigan Pier* he makes a similar aesthetic (and patriotic) appeal. He notes that English apples lie rotting under the trees because consumers prefer an American or Australian apple, 'a lump of highly-coloured cotton wool', which has the shine of a machine-made object, and because 'the palate is almost a dead organ' (*WP*, ch. 12).

Orwell does not need to tie up the ending of this novel in the way he felt compelled to do in *Burmese Days*. Indeed there are no strands of plot to tie up. The circular development, which returns Bowling to where he began, and changes nothing, shows that the novel is more an extended meditation about the state of England than a story about characters who progress in some way.

Orwell's chief purpose is to attack complacency and provoke the reader into realising that not only is war with Germany imminent, but also that England's democracy is weak, and that, if she were to be defeated, Fascism in the 'after-war' might take root. But Bowling's pessimistic prophecies are disregarded, and all the people he knows or meets are too stupid or limited to give us any hope. Far from proposing a political solution to the problem he describes, Bowling, like Gordon Comstock, almost seems to relish the prospect of the inevitable smash-up. At the end of the novel, recalling his earlier 'prophetic mood', Bowling says, 'the old life's finished, and to go about looking for it is just a waste of time' (Part Four, ch. 6), and he seems to have nothing to look forward to but the fulfilment of his prophecy.

In *Wigan Pier* Orwell had debated the effect of modern technology (which he called 'the machine') on English civilisation, but finally argued that, despite its tendency to equate mechanisation with progress, socialism was the only way to promote social equality and save England from Fascism. In *Coming Up for Air* his view of England is much less optimistic and more conservative. He continues to attack the machine, which Bowling associates with the deterioration of food, houses, and the natural environment, and the increase of the destructive power of modern weapons. We can see from the examples he chooses on which to base his arguments that Orwell valued differences, in people, cultures, objects, and cherished the idea of the inherent appropriateness, the enduring 'comeliness' of traditional practices. He could not bear the fact that, although it brings greater wealth, industrialisation inevitably makes society and culture more homogeneous. He could not reconcile (as who can?) the benefits of technology with its capacity to harm and pollute.

Isaac Rosenfeld, referring to this contradiction in Orwell between the desire for social revolution and respect for cultural continuity, said that he was 'a radical in politics and a conservative in feeling'.[48] Orwell's novels express his dismay at the changes in the English countryside and his doubts about England's future. Although in essays and patriotic propaganda pieces he celebrated the aspects of England he loved, and argued that a socialist revolution was compatible with a decent way of life, in the novels from *Keep the Aspidistra Flying* onwards he expressed more forcefully the idea that humane values probably will be defeated ('It's all going to happen'), and that nothing is destined to get better.

7

Animal Farm: An Allegory of Revolution

So far is it from being true that men are naturally equal, that no two people can be half an hour together, but one shall acquire an evident superiority over the other.

Samuel Johnson, quoted in James Boswell, *Life of Johnson*

In spite of Orwell's well-known opposition to continued British rule in India (where *Burmese Days* was banned) he was hired in August 1941 to produce programmes for the Indian section of the BBC's Eastern Service, to counter Japanese and German radio propaganda. Two million Indian volunteer troops were fighting on the British side, and the BBC's task was to maintain Indian support. For more than two years Orwell prepared weekly news bulletins, commissioned cultural talks and discussions, adapted stories, wrote dialogues and reviews. Because paper was in short supply, newspapers and magazines, the outlets for Orwell's work, were very restricted. Broadcasting allowed him to keep up his political comment and literary journalism. W. J. West has convincingly suggested that Orwell's experience in radio adaptation and in condensing, simplifying and arranging information for propaganda purposes largely accounts for the success of *Animal Farm* – its speed of composition (Orwell completed it in three months, after leaving the BBC in November 1943), its clarity and conciseness, its universality of appeal, its radically different form from any of Orwell's previous work.[49]

'*Animal Farm*', Orwell wrote, 'was the first book in which I tried, with full consciousness of what I was doing, to fuse political purpose and artistic purpose into one whole' (*CEJL*, 1.7). In his preface to the Ukrainian edition, published in 1947, Orwell said that he wanted to write the book in a simple language because

101

he wanted to tell ordinary English people, who had enjoyed a tradition of justice and liberty for centuries, what a totalitarian system was like. His experience in Spain had shown him 'how easily totalitarian propaganda can control the opinion of enlightened people in democratic countries' and he wrote the book to destroy the 'Soviet myth' that Russia was a truly socialist society (*CEJL*, 3.404).

In the 1930s European intellectuals idealised the Soviet Union. Even E. M. Forster, a relatively non-political writer, commented in an essay of 1934, 'no political creed except communism offers an intelligent man any hope'.[50] Throughout the 1930s Orwell had been sceptical about the Soviet version of current events in Russia; in Spain he saw Spanish Communists, directed by Moscow, betray their allies. In the late 1930s news reached the West of the infamous Purge Trials, which took the lives of three million people and sent countless others to forced labour camps in order to make Stalin's power absolute. In 1939 Stalin signed a non-aggression pact with Hitler, which allowed the Germans to overrun Poland and Czechoslovakia. Orwell's indignant reaction to these events provoked him to write this powerful pamphlet.

THE GENRE OF *ANIMAL FARM*

Orwell particularly valued the vigorous, colourful and concrete style of pamphlets and wanted to revive the genre. *Animal Farm* was his contribution to the English tradition of Utopian pamphlets, which originated in Thomas More's *Utopia* (1516). Like *Utopia*, *Animal Farm* is brief, light and witty, but has a serious purpose. More's pamphlet attacked the monarch's excessive power and the cruel dispossession of tenant-farmers by the lords who enclosed lands for sheep-grazing; Orwell's attacks the injustice of the Soviet regime and seeks to correct Western misconceptions about Soviet Communism.

More invented the device of satirising contemporary society by contrasting it with a traveller's account of a distant country. His narrator talks to Raphael Hythloday, who has just returned from Utopia (a name derived from the Greek, meaning 'no place' or 'nowhere'). In contrast to the majority of Englishmen, who suffer poverty and constant war, the Utopians are rational and kind, own everything in common and share everything equally.

War, envy, greed and pursuit of personal riches or power are unknown.

More's narrator remarks sceptically that he 'cannot conceive of authority among men that are equal to one another in all things'.[51] He cannot imagine a world where no one has greater status or wealth than anyone else. More raised the fundamental question, which Orwell took up centuries later, of whether it is possible for men to live together fairly, justly and equally. More's answer is ethical: that there is no point in changing our social system unless we change our morality; his pamphlet urges us to take responsibility for improving our society. While More's Utopia is totally imaginary, Orwell's Animal Farm is based on the first thirty years of the Soviet Union, a real society pursuing the ideal of equality. His book argues that this kind of society hasn't worked, and couldn't.

Orwell said that Jonathan Swift's *Gulliver's Travels* (1726) 'has meant more to me than any other book ever written'.[52] Far longer and more complex than *Utopia*, it uses the same device of a traveller's tales to attack contemporary society, but the various places Gulliver visits are satiric renderings of aspects of English society. Orwell's Animal Farm, like Swift's Lilliput and Blefuscu, is a coded satiric portrait of a real society, an anti-utopia which, by castigating real evils, suggests what society ought to be like.

Orwell probably took a hint from the final part of *Gulliver's Travels*, Book IV, where Gulliver encounters a society formed by a superior species of horse, the Houyhnhnms, who are able to talk and conduct their lives rationally (in contrast to the savage Yahoos nearby, who, to his horror, turn out to be ape-like humans). This comparison between men and animals, in which animals are superior, may have suggested the form of Orwell's pamphlet. Orwell was also familiar with Wells's *Island of Dr Moreau*, a science-fiction novel about a doctor who turns animals into men. But this novel uses the natural goodness of animals as a contrast to the evil of modern scientific man. Unlike Swift and Wells, Orwell uses animals to symbolise human characters.

THE POLITICAL ALLEGORY

Orwell's critique of Soviet Communism is a beast-fable, a satiric form in which animals are used to represent human vice and folly. Chaucer's 'Nun's Priest's Tale', one of the *Canterbury Tales*, is an early example in English. On one level Chaucer's tale is a comic farmyard tale of a proud cock, Chanticleer, who falls prey to the fox and manages to escape; on another it is a witty and learned essay on the significance of dreams; on another, and more serious, level it is an allegory of the Fall of Man, in which Chanticleer represents Adam being tempted by the Devil. *Animal Farm*, a brief, concentrated satire, subtitled 'A Fairy Story', can also be read on the simple level of plot and character. It is an entertaining, witty tale of a farm whose oppressed animals, capable of speech and reason, overcome a cruel master and set up a revolutionary government. They are betrayed by the evil power-hungry pigs, especially by their leader, Napoleon, and forced to return to their former servitude. Only the leadership has changed. On another, more serious level, of course, it is a political allegory, a symbolic tale where all the events and characters represent events and characters in Russian history since 1917,[53] in which 'the interplay between surface action and inner meaning is everything'.[54] Orwell's deeper purpose is to teach a political lesson.

As he noted in his Ukrainian preface, Orwell used actual historical events to construct his story, but rearranged them to fit his plot. Manor Farm is Russia, Mr Jones the Tsar, the pigs the Bolsheviks who led the revolution. The humans represent the ruling class, the animals the workers and peasants. Old Major, the white boar who inspires the rebellion in the first chapter, stands for a combination of Marx, the chief theorist, and Lenin, the actual leader. Orwell makes Old Major a character whose motives are pure and idealistic, to emphasise the positive goals of the revolution, and makes him die before the rebellion itself. In actuality Lenin died in 1924, well after the revolution. Lenin himself set up the machinery of political terror which Stalin took over. The power struggle between Stalin and Trotsky (which Orwell satirises in chapter 5) happened after Lenin's death, not immediately after the revolution, as Orwell's account suggests.

The *Communist Manifesto* (1848) of Karl Marx and Friedrich Engels provided a theoretical basis for the revolutionary movements springing up in Europe in the latter part of the nineteenth century. Marx interpreted all history as the history of class struggle, arguing that the capitalist classes, or bourgeoisie, the owners of the means of production, are inevitably opposed to the interests of the wage-earning labourers, or proletariat, whom they exploit. This eternal conflict can only be resolved by revolution, when workers take over the means of production, share the fruits of their labours equally, and set up 'the dictatorship of the proletariat'. Marx's ideal was an international brotherhood of workers (for he believed that the interests of the working classes of all nations would unite them, causing them to cross barriers of race and culture, against the common enemy) and a future classless society. Old Major's speech in the first chapter parodies the ideas of the *Communist Manifesto*. He says: 'Only get rid of Man, and the produce of our labour would be our own.' Their goal should be the 'overthrow of the human race': in the coming struggle 'All men are enemies. All animals are comrades.' In chapter 3 'everyone worked according to his capacity', an echo of the Marxist slogan, 'From each according to his abilities, to each according to his needs.'

Each animal stands for a precise figure or representative type. The pigs, who can read and write and organise, are the Bolshevik intellectuals who came to dominate the vast Soviet bureaucracy. Napoleon is Stalin, the select group around him the Politburo, Snowball is Trotsky, and Squealer represents the propagandists of the regime. The pigs enjoy the privileges of belonging to the new ruling class (special food, shorter working hours), but also suffer the consequences of questioning Napoleon's policies.

The other animals represent various types of common people. Boxer the carthorse (whose name suggests the Boxer Rebellion of 1900, when revolutionaries tried to expel foreigners from China), is the decent working man, fired by enthusiasm for the egalitarian ideal, working overtime in the factories or on the land, willing to die to defend his country; Clover is the eternal, motherly working woman of the people. Molly, the unreliable, frivolous mare, represents the White Russians who opposed the revolution and fled the country; the dogs are the vast army of secret police who maintain Stalin in power; the sheep are the ignorant public who repeat the latest propaganda without thinking and who can be made to turn up to 'spontaneous demonstrations' in support of Napoleon's plans. Moses, the raven, represents the opportunist Church. He flies off after Mr Jones, but returns later, and continues to preach about the Sugarcandy Mountain (or heaven), but the pigs' propaganda obliterates any lingering belief. Benjamin the donkey, the cynical but powerless average man, never believes in the glorious future to come, and is always alert to every betrayal.

Orwell's allegory is comic in its detailed parallels: the hoof and horn is clearly the hammer and sickle, the Communist party emblem; 'Beasts of England' is a parody of the 'Internationale', the party song; the Order of the Green Banner is the Order of Lenin, and the other first- and second-class awards spoof the fondness of Soviet Russia for awarding medals, for everything from exceeding one's quota on the assembly line or in the harvest to bearing a great many children. The poem in praise of Napoleon imitates the sycophantic verses and the mass of paintings and sculptures turned out to glorify Stalin. In chapter 8, Squealer's presentation of impressive figures to show that food production had gone up, and the thin layer of grain sprinkled over the sacks to deceive Whymper, the agent, correspond to the well-known practice in totalitarian regimes of falsifying figures to project a positive image abroad.

Each event of the story has a historical parallel. The Rebellion in chapter 2 is the October 1917 Revolution, the Battle of the Cowshed in chapter 4 the subsequent Civil War. Mr Jones and the farmers represent the loyalist Russians and foreign forces who tried, but failed, to dislodge the Bolsheviks. The hens' revolt in chapter 7 stands for the brutally suppressed 1921 mutiny of the sailors at Kronstadt, which challenged the new regime to release political prisoners and grant freedoms of speech and the press. Napoleon's deal with Whymper, who trades the farm's produce at Willingdon market, represents Russia's 1922 Treaty of Rapallo with Germany. Orwell emphasises Napoleon's decision to trade because it breaks the First Commandment, that 'whatever goes upon two legs is an enemy'. Official Soviet policy was hostile to Germany, a militaristic, capitalist nation, but the Treaty revealed that the Communist regime had been trading arms and heavy machinery, and would continue to do so.

Mr Frederick of 'Pinchfield', renowned for his cruelty to animals and for appropriating others' land, represents Hitler, though his name also suggests the despotic eighteenth-century Prussian king Frederick the Great. Mr Pilkington of 'Foxwood' stands for Churchill and England, a country dominated by the fox-hunting upper classes. The Windmill stands for the first Five-Year Plan of 1928, which called for rapid industrialisation and collectivisation of agriculture. Its destruction in a storm in chapter 6 symbolises the grim failure of this policy. Chapter 7 describes in symbolic terms the famine and starvation which followed. The hens' revolt stands for the peasants' bitter resistance to collective farming, when they burned their crops and slaughtered their animals. The animals' false confessions in chapter 7 are the Purge Trials of the late 1930s. The false banknotes given by Frederick for the corn represent Hilter's betrayal of the Nazi–Soviet Pact of 1939, and the second destruction of the Windmill, by Frederick's men, is the Nazi invasion of Russia in 1941. The last chapter brings Orwell up to the date of the book's composition. He ends with a satiric portrait of the Teheran Conference of 1943, the meeting of Churchill, Roosevelt and Stalin, who are now allies. The quarrel over cheating at cards predicts the falling-out of the superpowers as soon as the war ended.

Animal Farm's apparent simplicity disguises Orwell's ingenuity in fitting all these complex historical events into a simple and persuasive plot. Like the three wishes of a fairy tale, the Seven Commandments are an effective structural device. Their stage-by-stage alteration charts the pigs' progressive rise to power and lends the narrative a tragic inevitability. This change also symbolises a key theme of the book: the totalitarian falsification of history. The pigs' gradual acquisition of privileges – apples, milk, house, whisky, beer, clothes – leads to the final identification of pig and human, Communist and capitalist.

The plot's circular movement, which returns the animals to conditions very like those in the beginning, provides occasions for vivid irony. In the first chapter they lament their forced labour and poor food, but by chapter 6 they are starving, and are forced to work once more. In chapter 1 Old Major predicts that one day Jones will send Boxer to the knacker, and in chapter 9 Napoleon fulfils the prophecy by sending him to the slaughterhouse. In chapter 7, when various animals falsely confess their crimes and are summarily executed by the dogs, 'the air was heavy with the smell of blood, which had been unknown there since the expulsion of Jones'. These ironies all emphasise the tragic failure of the revolution, and support Benjamin's view that 'life would go on as it had always gone on – that is, badly' (ch. 5).

Though all the characters are types, Orwell differentiates the two most important figures, Napoleon and Snowball, so that they resemble their real-life counterparts both in the broad lines of their characterisation and in their two major disagreements. Like Stalin, Napoleon 'has a reputation for getting his own way' (ch. 2), takes charge of indoctrinating the young, sets up an elaborate propaganda machine, cultivates an image of omnipotent, charismatic power (a 'personality cult'), surrounding himself with bodyguards and fawning attendants. Like Trotsky, Snowball is an intellectual, who quickly researches a topic and formulates plans; he is a persuasive orator, but fails to wrest the leadership from Napoleon.

Napoleon and Snowball's quarrel over the Windmill represents their dispute over what should take priority in developing the Soviet Union. Stalin wanted to collectivise agriculture, Trotsky was for developing industry. Ultimately Stalin adopted both programmes in his first Five-Year Plan, just as Napoleon derides Snowball's plans, then uses them as his own. Their most fundamental disagreement was whether to try to spread the revolution to other countries, as classical Marxism dictated, or confine themselves to making a socialist state in Russia. Napoleon argues for the latter, saying that the animals must arm themselves to protect their new leadership, Snowball that they must send more pigeons into neighbouring farms to spread the news about the revolution. Just as Stalin abandoned the idea of world revolution, so at the end Napoleon assures the farmers that he will not spread rebellion among their animals.

Expelled from the Politburo in 1925, Trotsky went into exile in 1929 and was considered a heretic. His historical role was altered, his face cut out of group photographs of the leaders of the revolution; in Russia he was denounced as a traitor and conspirator and in 1940 he was assassinated in Mexico City by a Stalinist agent. Similarly, Snowball is blamed for everything that goes wrong in Animal Farm, and the animals are persuaded that he was a traitor from the beginning. Orwell did not share the view (of Isaac Deutscher and followers of Trotsky) that the revolution would have turned out differently had Trotsky, and not Stalin, become the leader after Lenin's death. Orwell makes Snowball equally bloodthirsty and immoral. In chapter 4, as Boxer grieves over the apparent death of the stableboy whom he has kicked in the battle, Snowball urges him not to be sentimental, because 'the only good human being is a dead one'. Trotsky defended the killing of the Tsar's children, on the grounds that the murderers acted on behalf of the proletariat.[55]

It has been said that the very act of reducing human characters to animals implies a pessimistic view of man, and that in *Animal Farm* the satiric vision is close to the tragic.[56] Orwell turns elements of comedy into scenes of tragic horror. In chapter 5, for example, Napoleon comically lifts his leg to urinate on Snowball's plans. But shortly afterwards he summons the dogs and orders them to rip out the throats of those who confess their disloyalty. In one instance Napoleon's contempt is amusing, in the next horrifying. Boxer's characteristics are similarly double-edged. In chapter 3 his earnest dimwittedness contrasts amusingly with the pigs' sharpness: while he is labouring to master the alphabet, and can't get past D, Snowball is engaging in parody-dialectic, explaining that birds can be included in the rule that 'Four legs good, two legs bad', since 'A bird's wing ... is an organ of propulsion and not of manipulation.' But Boxer's trusting simplicity also leads to his death, in one of the most moving scenes in the book.

The beast-fable is not only a device that allows Orwell's serious message to be intelligible on two levels; the use of animal to represent man is basic to his whole theme. We can readily grasp that animals are oppressed and feel it is wrong to exploit them and betray their trust. Orwell counts on our common assumptions about particular species to suggest his meaning. The sheep and their bleating are perfect metaphors for a gullible public, ever ready to accept policies and repeat rumours as truth. We commonly believe pigs are greedy and savage, even to the point of devouring their young. Orwell also uses the natural animosity of cats to sparrows, dogs to rats, to suggest the social and ethnic conflicts which belie Marx's dictum that workers' common interests outweigh differences of race and nationhood. And, most central to his theme, their 'short animal lives' suggests the book's tragic vision: that the passivity and ignorance of ordinary people allows an evil leadership to stay in power.

Orwell wanted his central figure to typify the modern dictator, whose lust for power is pathological and inhuman. Napoleon's swift, secret cruelty makes the other animals seem all too human in comparison. In a review of Hitler's *Mein Kampf*, Orwell described Napoleon, Hitler and Stalin as the quintessential modern dictators, who stayed in power for similar reasons: 'All three of the great dictators have enhanced their power by imposing intolerable burdens on their peoples' (*CEJL*, 2.14). To create

Napoleon, Orwell combines aspects of both Stalin and Hitler (just as the totalitarian society in *Nineteen Eighty-Four* shares characteristics of both Stalinist Russia and Nazi Germany). The animals make enormous sacrifices to complete the Windmill, only to find that it is used to grind corn (for trade), not to make their lives easier, as Snowball had promised. Napoleon 'denounced such ideas as contrary to the spirit of Animalism. The truest happiness, he said, lay in working hard and living frugally' (ch. 10). This maxim sounds an ironic echo of the Nazi slogan 'Arbeit macht frei' ('Work liberates'), which decorated the entrance to Auschwitz. The knacker's van which carries Boxer off to the slaughterhouse, and the deception used to induce him to enter it, recall the deportations of Jews to the death-camps, and the mobile extermination vans used to round up and murder small groups of villagers. By making Napoleon a boar Orwell also drew on the literary and historical associations of Shakespeare's *Richard III*, the literary archetype of the ugly, charismatic, absolutist schemer, whose heraldic emblem was the boar.[57]

The beast-fable form not only allowed Orwell to convey a complex message in simple terms, but was also admirably suited to his habits as a writer: his tendency to reduce characters to type, to see society as groups of competing economic interests; his narrator's detachment from the characters; his preference for grammatically simple sentences and unpretentious vocabulary. The prose succeeds brilliantly at balancing entertainment and argument because Orwell blends homely, even clichéd, language with sophisticated diction. In chapter 3, for example, 'the work of the farm went like clockwork' when the animals were in charge; into this simple fabric Orwell inserts a word with Marxist overtones: 'with the worthless *parasitical* human beings gone there was more for everyone to eat'. The context makes the word perfectly comprehensible to someone who does not know its meaning, yet if we know the word we can appreciate an additional layer of meaning – the suggestion that the animals have been indoctrinated with the Marxist view of capitalists as parasites, who own the means of production but do no work. The pleasure of reading *Animal Farm* lies in recognising the double meanings, the political and historical parallels, in the story.

In a book where distortion of language is an important theme, every word counts. Orwell's simple language points out the absurd contradictions between public political statements and private perceptions of their meaning. In chapter 6 all extra work is voluntary, but animals who refuse to do it lose half their rations; in chapter 9 Squealer announces a 'readjustment' of rations, instead of the more accurate 'reduction'. This doubletalk culminates in the last chapter, when the Commandments are reduced to one: 'All animals are equal' now has added to it 'but some are more equal than others'. The comic effect of these verbal distinctions does not diminish the tragedy of the revolution betrayed.

ORWELL'S CRITIQUE OF MARX

Marx's most revolutionary idea is that no social form is unalterable. Since all monarchies, class systems, governments are made by man, they can be destroyed and replaced by a better, fairer system, in which men would no longer be exploited. Marx thought it historically inevitable that workers would revolt, seize the means of production, and set up a centralised government, which he termed, paradoxically, a 'dictatorship of the proletariat'. The government of the Soviet Union, however, was ruled by a new élite, a collective oligarchy, some of whom were derived from the proletariat. Orwell described such governments as 'a sham covering a new form of class-privilege' (*CEJL*, 3.320).

Orwell had always been fascinated by the corrupting effects of power and the relative weakness of good and decent people in the face of evil intelligence. In *Animal Farm* Orwell argues that, however desirable the ideal, man's instinct for power makes the classless society impossible. In his allegory, a Marxist revolution is doomed to fail, because it grants power, once again, to a select few. Major's speech 'had given to *the more intelligent animals* ... a completely different outlook on life'.

To oppose Marx, Orwell turned to a classic seventeenth-century work of political philosophy, Thomas Hobbes's *Leviathan* (1651). A fiercely anti-revolutionary writer, Hobbes presents views of man and politics diametrically opposed to those of Marx. According to Hobbes, the life of man is 'solitary, poor, nasty, brutish and short', and all human beings are inclined to 'a perpetual and restless desire after power, which ceaseth only in death' (*Leviathan*, Book 1, ch. 11). Far from seeing men as capable of creating a new society to ensure their equality, Hobbes thought that only fear of death made men control their lust for power sufficiently to band together to form a commonwealth, an artificial machine to protect them from their enemies. For Hobbes, the one requirement of government, of whatever kind, was that it be strong enough to hold warring factions in check. He considered it inevitable that society be divided into social classes.

There are several important echoes of Hobbes in *Animal Farm*. Ironically, Marx–Major paraphrases Hobbes in the first chapter, when he says, 'our lives are miserable, laborious, and short'. In the last chapter, when the animals can no longer remember the promises of the revolution, Benjamin expresses the Hobbesian opinion that 'hunger, hardship and disappointment . . . [are] the unalterable law of life'. Alone of all the animals, Benjamin refuses either to hope or be disappointed, and his commentary often suggests a Swiftian cynicism, such as when he refuses to read, on the ground that there is nothing worth reading. This choice turns out to be the wise one, when we consider how the written word has been manipulated by the pigs.

But we should not assume that Benjamin's voice represents Orwell's. Orwell did not agree with Hobbes's political philosophy, nor did he, like Swift, find mankind ultimately disgusting. He simply believed that the rise of Russian totalitarianism could best be explained by Hobbes's theory, rather than by Marx's. Orwell summed up his attitude to revolution in the preface to a collection of British pamphlets:

> The most encouraging fact about revolutionary activity is that, although it always fails, it always continues. The vision of a world of free and equal human beings, living together in a state of brotherhood – in one age it is called the Kingdom of Heaven, in another the classless society – never materialises, but the belief in it never seems to die out.[58]

Orwell had great difficulty publishing *Animal Farm*, which he completed in February 1943, for Russia had become an ally in the war against Germany, and was suffering heavy losses. Though he praised the style and compared it to Swift, T. S. Eliot, a director of Faber, spoke for most publishers when he rejected it because 'we have no conviction that this is the right point of view from which to criticise the political situation at the present time'. He told Orwell that he found the ending unsatisfactory because 'your pigs are far more intellectual than the other animals, and therefore the best qualified to run the farm', and that clearly all that was needed was 'more public-spirited pigs',[59] though, as Orwell's book shows, revolutionary leaders are rarely public-spirited. Finally published in August 1945, *Animal Farm* was given the highest praise by Graham Greene and by Edmund Wilson, but some critics refused to accept the validity of Orwell's attack on Soviet Communism. Cyril Connolly defended Russia, asserting that 'despite a police system which we should find intolerable, the masses are happy, and . . . great strides in material progress have been made'.[60] Northrop Frye considered the allegory superficial, and sneered at the ending, asserting that the moral of the book is 'the reactionary bromide' that 'you can't change human nature'.[61] But Orwell's book does not pretend to be a probing analysis of Russian Communism. His purpose was to expose the totalitarian nature of the Russian government in as simple and effective a form as possible, and in this he succeeded. It is a cautionary tale, but what it suggests about power and revolution is not reducible to a formula.

As for the criticism that Orwell's satire is exaggerated, the book's continued popularity (in illegal editions) in Eastern Europe shows that his satire is as accurate as it is enduring. As recently as September 1987, customs officials at the Moscow International Book Fair cleared the British exhibitors' shelves of *Animal Farm*. There can be no better certification of its truth.

8

Nineteen Eighty-Four: An Anti-Utopia

The mass of the people never get the chance to bring their innate decency into the control of affairs, so that one is almost driven to the cynical thought that men are only decent when they are powerless.

CEJL, 1.336

In his socialist pamphlet *The Lion and the Unicorn* (1941), Orwell contrasted the defeatist attitudes of middle-class intellectuals, who flirted with Communism but had no intention of giving up their class privileges, with the instinctive patriotism and basic decency of the British working man (*CEJL*, 2.74). Later, in *The English People* (1944), he remarked that in England people could scarcely imagine 'the real totalitarian atmosphere, in which the state endeavours to control people's thoughts as well as their words' (*CEJL*, 3.12). And in an essay on his friend Arthur Koestler, a refugee from Fascist and Communist prisons, he noted that England had no 'concentration camp literature', like Koestler's *Darkness at Noon* (1941), a novel that describes the arrest, torture and forced confession of a Soviet commissar.

Nineteen Eighty-Four, Orwell's most ambitious and complex novel, brings home to England the experience of Koestler and countless others who suffered in the totalitarian regimes of Eastern Europe. He thought of writing it as early as 1940, during the bleak years of the war with Germany, and completed it in 1948, as the Cold War with Russia was beginning. Both a work of fiction and an anti-utopian political pamphlet, the novel describes a future England, no longer the head of an Empire, but as 'Airstrip One', a grimy, run-down outpost of Oceania, a vast totalitarian system which includes North America and

114

the British Empire, and spans a third of the globe. Orwell describes the worst possible 'state of England' to shock his audience into imagining what it would be like to live under a totalitarian government, and to urge them to preserve their traditional rights to privacy, freedom and obedience to the rule of law. Throughout the novel, but especially through the character of O'Brien, in Part Three, Orwell continues to attack the left-wing intellectuals he believed were prepared to abandon democratic principles and to accept Communist dictatorship in exchange for power and privilege, and he dramatises the moral differences between the intellectuals and the 'proles'.

Orwell's last book reworks the settings and characters of his earlier fiction. The hero's struggles to achieve integrity supply the plot and the narrator's ironic point of view. Lonely, guilty, lustful and obsessed with the past, Winston Smith feels as alienated from his colleagues at the Ministry of Truth as John Flory in the European Club at Kyauktada, as out of sympathy with the values of his society as Gordon Comstock or George Bowling. From the first paragraph the atmosphere of *Nineteen Eighty-Four* recalls Orwell's earlier shabby urban settings. Nondescript, seedy, thirty-nine years old, Winston enters Victory Mansions (where the hallway smells of boiled cabbage) pursued by a 'vile wind' and a 'swirl of gritty dust'. Like Gordon Comstock, he is going up to a dreary room; later in the ministry canteen he 'had only four cigarettes left' (Part One, ch. 5). He lives among bomb-craters and rubble, the aftermath of the universal 'smash-up' Comstock and Bowling had almost gleefully anticipated. The novel converts the social injustice, sexual repression and xenophobia of England in the 1930s into the rigid class system, sexual puritanism, and permanent state of war in Oceania. While Comstock and Bowling are 'little men' whose ambitions are soon dampened by the inevitable compromise with ordinary life, Winston's conformity is achieved through indoctrination, surveillance and torture.

Nineteen Eighty-Four combines the political theme and polemic purpose of *Animal Farm* with the human characters of the social novel. The citizens of Airstrip One suffer the same indignities as the animals: physical deprivation and chronic shortages; a country constantly at war; repetitive propaganda to manipulate public opinion; the deliberate falsification of history and systematic obliteration of the past; and ruthless extermination of political opposition. The first part of the novel is a satiric sketch of Winston's life and especially his job at the Ministry of Truth. The second part begins with his first conversation with Julia, describes the progress of their love affair, Winston's growing belief in the existence of a secret movement to overthrow Big Brother and his contact with O'Brien, and ends with their dramatic arrest. The last part, set almost entirely within the walls of the Ministry of Love, describes Winston's brainwashing and final defeat.

THE LITERARY SOURCES

Though Orwell admired the surrealistic effects and imaginative play with form and language of modernist writers, he had always acknowledged his own imaginative and technical limitations. In *Nineteen Eighty-Four*, however, Orwell's polemic purpose led him to combine genres and styles in a daring and original way. His attack on totalitarian systems is far more complex than in *Animal Farm*, blending realism, parody (including fake 'documents') and satire. Orwell used documentary realism to construct a far more detailed attack on Fascist and Communist governments than was possible in the beast-fable, and the future setting released him from conventional realism's limitations.

For the form of his novel, Orwell drew on the rich satiric tradition of English utopian fiction. Julia's work on the novel-writing machines suggests the machines in Book Two of *Gulliver's Travels*. His title, which reverses the last two digits of its year of composition, hinting that his target is to attack present society as much as to warn about the future, imitates the title of Samuel Butler's *Erewhon*, which is simply 'nowhere' spelled backwards (or nearly). But Orwell's chief models, which he both imitated and argued against, were Wells's scientific romances, Yevgeny Zamyatin's novel *We* (1923), and Aldous Huxley's *Brave New World* (1932).

In Wellsian futuristic novels, the hero, like the Sleeper of *When the Sleeper Awakes* (1899), is usually transported by some fantastic means to a remote time or place (in this case he sleeps for two hundred years, and wakes in about 2100). Dismayed by the barbarous world he is in, he meets a powerful figure who explains the society to him. Finally he is able either to return to his original world, or to attempt, perhaps unsuccessfully, to fight against conditions in the new. *In the Days of the Comet* (1906), a blend of social novel and romantic utopia, is an optimistic version of this pattern. The hero angrily denounces the state of England, where there are 'two great informal divisions of human beings – the Secure and the Insecure' (Book 1, ch. 3). The arrival of a mysterious comet, however, begins a new dawn of peace and equality, and the hero inherits a new and better world.

The plot of *Nineteen Eighty-Four* is an ironic variant of the Wellsian pattern. Winston and Julia exist in the future, try to escape into the atmosphere of the past, and are harshly wrenched back to the future. The hero has no compensatory revelation or miraculous escape. As one critic has noted, Winston is a product of the future society and at the same time represents the world of the author and the reader. The powerful figure who answers his questions about the principles of society is the evil O'Brien, who both enlightens and dooms him.[62]

Wells's science fiction debates the question of how modern man will use advances in science and technology, and his many works give both optimistic and pessimistic answers. Zamyatin, a Russian author who was himself influenced by Wells, inspired Orwell to create an oppressive imaginary society ruled by terror. In *We*, a satire on tendencies in post-revolutionary Russia, people have been reduced to numbers and live in glass houses so that they can be observed by the political police, or Guardians. The ironically-named Benefactor, whose principle is that freedom makes people unhappy, rules by terror and cruelty, beheading rebels in public. The hero, D-503, falls in love, conspires to overthrow the Benefactor, is arrested, is given an operation to remove his imagination, and betrays his co-conspirators.

When Orwell reviewed *We* he noted the many similarities between it and Huxley's *Brave New World*. He declared that its 'intuitive grasp of the irrational side of totalitarianism' made it superior to Huxley's novel (*CEJL*, 4.75). Orwell took his general plot from *We*, and used some of its features for Oceania (the Thought Police, for example). The themes of *Nineteen Eighty-Four*, however, have much more in common with *Brave New World*, even though Orwell's anti-utopia is based on terror, Huxley's on hedonism. Huxley's novel, like Zamyatin's, is set six hundred years hence. It depicts a society absolutely controlled by behavioural conditioning and drugs. All normal human feelings and functions are artificial, dependent on machines and chemicals. Sexual relationships are reduced to erotic play and promiscuity is required. The family no longer exists, because children are bred in bottles and 'decanted' in strictly controlled numbers and genetic types, according to their intended role. This world is observed by a Savage, the offspring of a member of a remote American Indian tribe (allowed to exist as a spectacle for weekend visitors) and a New World visitor who got lost on holiday and remained on the reservation. Although John Savage has been brought up in a degraded community, his mental outlook is based on the Shakespeare plays he has learned to read. Unlike any of the people he encounters in the World State, he has grown up with his own mother.

Though Huxley's novel is comic and witty, while Orwell's is darkly satiric and ultimately tragic, both novels mourn the potential cultural loss in a world governed either by comfort or cruelty. Both novels divide the workers and privileged class in roughly the same proportion: in *Brave New World* 'The optimum population is modelled on the iceberg – eight-ninths below the waterline, one-ninth above' (ch. 14). Both authors see the intellectuals as villains, who control the masses and despise them, yet practice self-censorship and conformity, and dread appearing to be different from others. Art and literature and the intellectual life are impossible, because imagination and knowledge of the past are forbidden, and because, as Huxley's World Controller remarks, 'you can't make tragedies without social instability. The world's stable now' (ch. 14). In both novels the government's goal is complete stasis: in Huxley, a *soma*-induced peace; in Orwell, a continuous state of war and paranoia.

Orwell called *Brave New World* 'a brilliant caricature of the present', but he maintained that 'hedonistic societies do not endure' because they are too boring, and that neither Wells nor Huxley had managed to create a convincing ruling class. Taking his inspiration from the recent despotic rule of Hitler and Stalin, Orwell created a regime he thought more plausible, one with 'a strict morality, a quasi-religious belief in itself' (*CEJL*, 2.30–31).

Nineteen Eighty-Four was published in 1949, as the Cold War was beginning. The novel's bleak, pessimistic ending made readers on both the Left and the Right take it as an attack on socialism in general and Communist Russia in particular, as well as a prophecy of what was in store for the West should Communist ideology spread. Even Orwell's own publisher, Fredric Warburg, on his first reading of the manuscript assumed that 'Ingsoc = English Socialism. This I take to be a deliberate and sadistic attack on socialism and socialist parties generally.' Warburg thought it would be worth 'a cool million votes to the conservative party' and considered getting a preface by Winston Churchill, the Prime Minister during the recent war, 'after whom its hero is named'.[63] An international bestseller, condensed in the *Reader's Digest*, translated into twenty-three languages, and distributed in translation in camps for displaced persons, many of them refugees from the new Stalinist regimes of Eastern Europe, *Nineteen Eighty-Four* seemed to cast Orwell in the unwilling role of anti-Communist propagandist.

Shortly after its publication Orwell defended his work from misinterpretation. In a letter to an American union leader Orwell asserted his continuing belief in socialism and defined his purpose in the novel:

> My recent novel is NOT intended as an attack on Socialism or on the British Labour Party (of which I am a supporter) but as a show-up of the perversions to which a centralised economy is liable and which have already been partly realised in Communism and Fascism.

He emphasised that the novel was a satire, and did not show what would, but what *could*, happen, and that 'totalitarian ideas have taken root in the minds of intellectuals'. He had tried to show what the logical consequences of those ideas might be, and had set the novel in Britain to show that 'totalitarianism, *if not fought against*, could triumph everywhere' (*CEJL*, 4.502).

THE SETTING: DOCUMENTARY REALISM AND SATIRE

The first two parts of *Nineteen Eighty-Four* show Orwell at his most Dickensian, where London itself, grotesque, squalid and menacing, is a palpable presence. In part, the city is London at war as his contemporary audience would recently remember it: the streets dark, full of holes and rubble, buildings crumbling, light and heat in short supply; lipstick, razor-blades and coffee are unobtainable except on the black market; food is tasteless and monotonous; air-raids are a constant danger. People carry identity-cards and ration-books; there are economy-drives run by volunteers, and posters reminding the public to watch out for spies. Government propaganda, statistical and patriotic, issues from the radio (or 'telescreen') and cinema newsreels.

Orwell exaggerates these everyday documentary details to create a disturbingly grotesque city of the future. The clock strikes thirteen as Winston escapes to his flat at lunch-time; inside the building the electricity is off as part of the preparation for Hate Week; as he mounts the stairs he feels pursued by the eyes of Big Brother, the remote and superhuman dictator, depicted on posters on every landing. Inside the flat a voice drones from the telescreen, and possibly the Thought Police are observing him; outside a Police Patrol flies by in a helicopter.

By 1984 London has been at war for more than thirty years, so long that most people know no other way of life (Winston remembers taking shelter as a child in tube-stations, a common practice during the Blitz). Despite propaganda films and daily rocket-bombs the enemy is unreal and victory remote. Winston knows that the enemy and ally have changed more than once, but he cannot be sure, for no objective historical record exists; in Oceania 'the enemy of the moment always represented absolute evil' (Part One, ch. 3) and jingoistic hatred is the order of the day. This is post-revolutionary London, drab, dingy and bare, where only fragments of the past remain. What has not been destroyed in the war, like St Clement Dane's church, has been defaced by ideology. The church of St Martin in the Fields, which now stands in Victory Square, houses a propaganda museum.

His colleagues are 'comrades', but humourless and cold, suspicious and fearful. These Londoners have no cockney wit or camaraderie, no pleasure in overcoming hardships together, because these hard times are permanent. 'What I mean to say, there is a war on', says Parsons, using the common, half-ironic wartime excuse, not for shortages, poor service and restrictions, but to justify his children's activities in the 'Spies'.

In a 'London Letter' in the spring of 1941 Orwell contrasted his position with that of the writers of the previous war: 'the conditions that made it possible for Joyce and Lawrence to do their best work during the war of 1914–18 (i.e. the consciousness that presently the world would be sane again) no longer exists' (*CEJL*, 2.54). *Nineteen Eighty-Four* expresses in its extremest form the key idea of Orwell's 1930s novels: that continuity with the past had been broken, and that the mad and destructive values of Fascism and Communism threatened to overwhelm the West. Specific features of life in Airstrip One parody well-known social phenomena of Nazi Germany or Russia of the 1930s and 1940s. The Two Minutes Hate and the vast Hate Week rally recall Hitler's Nuremberg rallies, where party speakers whipped up crowd hysteria. The Jewish Goldstein, one of the targets of hate, represents both the 'Zionist conspiracy' of Nazi ideology and the Russian 'renegade' Trotsky, Stalin's opponent and victim. Both regimes indoctrinated the young through youth groups: the 'Spies' of *Nineteen Eighty-Four* are modelled on the Hitler Youth and Soviet Young Pioneers (though the emphasis on hikes and clean thoughts suggests Baden-Powell's Boy Scout movement and the public-school ethos as well). Like Nazi and Soviet propaganda, the Party posters in *Nineteen Eighty-Four* celebrate a distinct physical type: 'tall, muscular youths and deep-bosomed maidens, blond-haired, vital, sunburnt, carefree', in contrast to the ill-assorted types Winston observes in the canteen (Part One, ch. 5).

Winston and Julia's Party uniform of blue overalls recalls not only the appearance of many English civilians during the war who worked in factories, but the Bolsheviks' adoption of working-class attire. The Three-Year Plans recall Stalin's Five-Year Plans. Orwell's imitation of Communist abbreviated compound words – Ingsoc, Miniluv, prolefeed – creates a comic and sinister effect. Like the omnipresent portraits of Lenin and Stalin in contemporary Russia, posters of Big Brother look down from every wall. In *Nineteen Eighty-Four* totalitarian practices common in modern Russia and China are used to discipline the population: forced labour; confessions extracted by torture; people disappear or are 'vapourized'; books opposed to the regime are destroyed and written records altered to fit current ideology; political orthodoxy, attendance at Party meetings and participation in collective activities are compulsory. Though Orwell seems to exaggerate the government's power to make the terror total – the two-way telescreen, the patrolling helicopters, the microphones hidden in trees and bushes – Winston's experience in Oceania is astonishingly parallel to the real-life accounts of terror and persecution in Stalinist Russia and Mao's China, many of which were not published until long after Orwell's death.[64] In Oceania, as in most of Eastern Europe until recently, the major part of the nation's resources are committed to arms and heavy industry, while food is scarce, housing and services inadequate and 'Nothing is efficient but the Thought Police' (Part Two, ch. 9).

Orwell derived his basic information from printed sources, film newsreels, or from the personal record of refugees such as Arthur Koestler, but he also drew imaginatively on his own practical experience. He had been a policeman, and knew how prisoners responded to confinement and punishment; he had been arrested (the white tile of Room 101 is very like the London cell described in 'Clink'). The starving man in prison with Winston in Part Three and the sadistic treatment of the man who tries to help him, the description of the convoy of shattered prisoners of war, were probably derived from what he observed as a reporter in Germany in February and March 1945.[65] Orwell disturbs us by domesticating terror and cruelty, by superimposing a totalitarian system onto a recognisably English scene, and uses his flat, matter-of-fact documentary style to make the world he describes credible.

Just as Dickens attacked the legal system in *Bleak House*, so Orwell uses the Ministry of Truth to satirise both the Ministry of Information, the government department responsible for collecting and disseminating facts and monitoring the news, and the British Broadcasting Corporation, nominally independent but subject to Ministry of Information censorship in wartime. During the war the Ministry of Information was housed in the Senate House of the University of London, a multi-storeyed grey building, which Orwell converts into the glittering white pyramid towering over the rubble of Airstrip One. Winston's job at Minitrue satirises Orwell's own often tedious work of preparing news summaries and cultural programmes at the BBC. The Newspeak jargon of Winston's instructions is based on cablese, the shorthand language of messages conveyed by cable. In his diary entry for 23 July 1942, Orwell bitterly regretted being a part of the futile waste of skilled people on 'things which in fact don't help ... the war effort'. He deplored the expense of the thousands of support staff who 'have no real job but have found themselves a quiet niche and are sitting in it' pretending to produce broadcasts which are 'shot into the stratosphere' and have no effect (*CEJL*, 2.437). Winston notes this wasted effort when he wonders whether the man in the next cubicle is working on the same trivial alteration.

Orwell pokes grim fun at the BBC as government propaganda machine, exaggerating and multiplying its functions. The Records Department of Minitrue is purely an instrument of centralised government, with total control of all media. It is responsible for 'news, entertainment, education and the fine arts' (Part One, ch. 1), dispenses a daily stream of meaningless and inaccurate statistics, doctors the news to fit government policy, and produces the entire range of visual and verbal material, 'from a statue to a slogan' (Part One, ch. 4). All news, art, literature and education is propaganda, and each product is cynically designed for its audience. The lowest range of material is 'prole-feed': 'rubbishy newspapers', 'sensational five-cent novelettes, films oozing with sex'. The Pornosec department creates porno-graphic materials 'sent out in sealed packets and which no Party member was permitted to look at'.

Orwell's satire is double-edged, directed not only against Eastern Communism, but also against the way wartime restric-tions endangered democracy. His job at the BBC gave him insight into the dangers of government control of information, and the power of mass media to limit thought and debase culture. He is especially acute on the newly invented television. Nothing is more chilling in *Nineteen Eighty-Four* than the ubiquitous tele-screen, which dispenses non-news and non-music unceasingly, and which costs Winston much mental effort to blot out. (It is a sign of O'Brien's power that he can turn it off – but only for thirty minutes.)

After years of freelance journalism, Orwell's job at the BBC put him back into a snobbish hierarchy, and seems to have shar-pened his distaste for bureaucrats. Winston's colleagues in the canteen, satiric portraits of managerial types, gabble in mechani-cal professional jargon, contemptuous of the 'greasy prole' behind the counter. In a diary entry Orwell praised the army of char-women who sang together zestfully as they swept the hallways at the BBC in the early mornings, giving the place 'a quite differ-ent atmosphere' from later in the day, when the white-collar workers took over (*CEJL*, 2.430). The smug, 'duckspeaking' young man at a nearby table is an example of the automatic, non-thinking adherent of the Party, but is little different from any dogmatic 'intellectual' in the West. In true English style, Winston hardly knows his fellow workers, who are at their most totalitarian and their most English when they take care not to remark on Syme's absence the day after his 'disappearance'. By synthesising his observations of wartime life, especially at the BBC, and his knowledge of the Nazi and Soviet terror, Orwell created a subtle portrait of London as the centre of a police state.

THE HISTORICAL SETTING: ORWELL'S USE OF PARODY

To create the illusion of a future historical and political reality, Orwell invented several 'real' documents, which Winston either reads, like the school history textbook and *The Book*, or writes himself, such as his diary and the Newspeak memos. These, and the 'Appendix on Newspeak' (which stands outside the action of the novel proper and suggests that the whole text of the novel exists as a kind of historical document), not only convey the flavour of life in Oceania, but also contribute to the argument. The school textbook Winston reads, a parody of Marxist propaganda, reinforces his despair at the impossibility of ever knowing what life before the revolution was really like. It insists that London is 'now' beautiful, not dark, dirty and miserable, as it was 'then'; that now we have equality, while then people were poor and exploited. Because the Party paints a consistently false picture of *now*, it cannot be trusted to explain *then*. In Oceania no one believes anything announced by the authorities, yet everyone must appear to believe it. The textbook is an example of 'doublethink' at work.

The longest and most important of the documents is *The Book*, lent to Winston by O'Brien and purportedly written by the renegade Goldstein, the object of the Two Minutes Hate. The extracts from the book occupy the central position in the novel, and function in several ways: they give us an overview of historical events, the political structure of Oceania, and its relationship to the rest of the world, so that we can understand Winston's setting in time; they summarise the key ideas in the novel's critique of Marxist–Leninist ideology: the rewriting of history, the process of 'doublethink' to ensure orthodoxy, the continuous state of war between Oceania and other powers, the betrayal of socialist ideals and the emergence of a new, privileged class; at the same time the book focuses Winston's thoughts ('systematized what he knew already') and encourages him to believe in his own sanity.

The Book parodies the ideas of James Burnham, an American economist, whose work Orwell had reviewed. In *The Managerial Revolution* (1941), Burnham had predicted that a future global political and economic structure would emerge after the war, probably won by Germany, was over. According to Burnham, the world would be divided into three areas, centring around the major industrial cities. Capitalism would disappear, but would not be replaced by socialism. Governments of the future would be led by 'managers', a talented elite of businessmen, technicians and high-ranking soldiers, who would co-opt the talented into their organisation. Below this oligarchy the vast majority of the population would be virtual slaves, working to produce goods according to the master-plan of those in power. These ideas are rehearsed in 'Chapter Three' of *The Book*.

The broken-off 'Chapter One' draws on Burnham's belief that the division of society into three hierarchical classes is universal and inevitable, and that human action derives from self-interest and lust for power. In Burnham's relativistic view, there are no transcendent moral values, only the rules set up by the party that happens to be in power. Ability to maintain power is his sole criterion for judging any form of government. Burnham took as his models two modern systems he thought highly successful: Nazi Germany, for its managerial efficiency, territorial gains and use of slave labour; and the Soviet Union, for the way in which Marxist revolution was quickly succeeded by dictatorship and oligarchy.

In his 1946 pamphlet *James Burnham and the Managerial Revolution*, Orwell argued against Burnham's ideas and predictions. He agreed that socialism, despite its ideal of the brotherhood of man, had failed to supplant capitalism, but did not believe that this proved that man was totally selfish and power-seeking. Since Burnham had not established that political activity was any different from any other human activity, it was nonsense to reduce all human action to self-interest. Orwell thought that prosperity and education could continue to reduce class differences. He pointed out that, though Burnham pretended to be objective, his theories were motivated by power-worship, and that this had caused him to overestimate the longevity of the Nazi regime. Orwell maintained that democracy had many benefits, stated that 'slavery is no longer a stable basis for a society', and predicted that 'the Russian régime will either democratise itself, or perish' (*CEJL*, 4.180).

In *Nineteen Eighty-Four* he continued the attack by imagining what English society would be like under the system Burnham had described. Like many other countries, his England has been devasted by atomic bombs. The world is divided into three power zones, Oceania, Eurasia and Eastasia, each ruled by centralised authoritarian oligarchies. Orwell imagines that possession of atomic weapons has produced stalemate, and that each zone maintains its rigid 'Inner Party' in power by waging perpetual conventional warfare.

The Book parodies Burnham's economic theories and Trotsky's attacks on Stalin's rule in *The Revolution Betrayed*. Burnham provides the structure of Oceania, and Trotsky the criticism of it. According to Goldstein, the aim of Oceania is to 'use up the products of the machine without raising the standard of living', to preserve the power of the anonymous elite who hide behind the mask of Big Brother. Trotsky himself, of course, believed in the Marxist revolution and had played a bloody role in setting up the very rule of terror he later deplored. Orwell's Goldstein completely rejects Oceania, and exposes the whole structure as a means of maintaining a savage oligarchy in power. His *Book*, which we realise in Part Three is probably the product of O'Brien himself, or other Inner Party members, is designed to entrap Winston by confirming his view of the political system.

WINSTON SMITH: WRITING AS ETHICAL CHOICE

Orwell imagined Winston Smith as 'The Last Man in Europe' (his working title for the novel), the last believer in humane values in a totalitarian age. Smith, the commonest English surname, suggests his symbolic value; 'Winston' evokes the name of Churchill, whose patriotic appeals for 'blood, sweat and tears' urged the British public to make the sacrifices necessary to defeat the Germans. Winston's final defeat is an ironic echo of the earlier Winston's victory, and suggests a powerless post-war England, dwarfed and threatened by the great powers.

Orwell's expository methods here are the most sophisticated of any of his novels. As before the hero's life-story gives the book its time-frame, but rather than narrating the character's story before the action properly begins, Orwell reveals Winston's past through dreams and memories. The novel traces the attempts of a disoriented person to understand the true nature of his environment. Winston dimly remembers the atomic war, when the bomb fell on Colchester, and the chaos of the civil war which followed. In the mid-1950s, when Winston was ten years old, during the power struggle after the war, a totalitarian party had siezed power, and he lost his parents and sister in the ensuing purges. Unlike Rubashov, the hero of Koestler's *Darkness at Noon*, who is an old revolutionary Inner Party member, Winston knows no other life. Brought up in a camp for orphans, he is almost entirely a product of the new society. Winston's attempt to capture a true sense of the past not only creates his character and situation, but structures the entire novel.

Just as Orwell identifies Dorothy Hare by her social rank in *A Clergyman's Daughter*, so Winston is assigned his place in the social structure. In Oceania, the Inner Party, or ruling oligarchy (represented by O'Brien) is the top two per cent; the Outer Party, to which Winston and Julia belong, the next thirteen per cent, are the talented, trained technicians who are most closely supervised and controlled; the remaining eighty-five per cent are the Proles, the degraded, slave-like workers, who appear briefly but significantly in the novel. Orwell constructs the social framework not only to define the central character, but to describe how this society works. Winston's role as intellectual, Outer Party member, enables him to penetrate the mystique of government control, but also ensures his severe punishment.

Just as Orwell exaggerates features of normal life and aspects of totalitarian societies to create his setting and atmosphere, so he gives Winston more extreme characteristics of earlier heroes: loneliness, guilt, physical weakness, sexual repression and frustration, alienation from society, desire for spiritual and moral integrity. Like Flory, he regrets his schooldays when he sympathised with the victim, but joined the bullies; like Gordon Comstock, he feels guilty about the way he treated his family; like George Bowling, he loathes his frigid wife. But Winston's experiences are all more severe and agonising than his predecessors'. His memories are not of prep school, but of a children's camp where he was indoctrinated with Party ideology; he does not feel snobbish shame about his family, but guilt from having survived starvation or extermination; his wife Katharine's frigidity is considered normal by the Party, his own longings abnormal and illegal.

Orwell's idea of the writer's purpose and relationship to his audience, satirised earlier in Gordon Comstock in *Keep the Aspidistra Flying*, becomes tragic in *Nineteen Eighty-Four*. Like Gordon, Winston focuses his anxiety on his writing, but here writing for oneself is not a pointless pastime, but a dangerous act, a desperate attempt to maintain one's sanity in a deranged world. Orwell contrasts Winston's keeping a diary, a sacred act of privacy, to the elaborate construction of lies at the ministry. In his job he alters the records of the past to fit current Party policy, translates them into the severely restricted vocabulary of Newspeak, dictates his corrections into the speakwrite, and throws his drafts down the memory hole. In private, he writes on the creamy paper of an old diary with an old-fashioned pen and ink. The first kind of writing is mechanical, but the conventions of Newspeak can make it tricky and exhausting, like doing a puzzle. It is temporary, lasting only until the next 'correction'. The second is psychologically liberating, but also disturbing, setting off memories and dreams. It is meant to last, to be read and reread, and demands all the nuance of Oldspeak. The first is systematic lying, the second a passionate search for truth.

In a darkly satiric episode, Winston invents a heroic comrade Ogilvy to replace the discredited Withers, now an unperson, in a speech given by Big Brother the year before. Winston derives great satisfaction from his skill, imagination and grasp of Party jargon. Orwell contrasts the confident, bureaucratic and mindless attitude Winston needs to do this work with his panic at the blank sheet of paper, his poor handwriting, his mental and emotional confusion, when he starts writing for his own purposes.

In spite of shifting alliances, Party policy and military strategy must always appear consistent and infallible. Since Oceania has no permanent records and no code of law, 'day by day and almost minute by minute the past was brought up to date', because the Party believes that 'who controls the past, controls the future: who controls the present controls the past' (Part One, ch. 4). Initially Winston writes in his diary to preserve his mental health, to clarify the confused 'interminable monologue' in his head. He wants to believe in order and truth, yet lives in a world where such absolutes are forbidden. The Party determines what the truth will be. Winston feels the familiar hysteria and rage during the hate, but realises that his emotions could be as easily directed against Big Brother as against Goldstein. Winston is manipulated by the system, and yet, in his role of Outer Party intellectual worker, he is part of the system which manipulates others.

Because the Party seeks absolute power, its goal is complete conformity. Any deviation is 'thoughtcrime'. Since the Party's decisions, no matter how irrational, may never be questioned, all Party members have to bear the burden of practising 'double-think', the ability 'to hold simultaneously two opinions which cancel each other out' (Part One, ch. 3), which Goldstein's *Book* calls 'controlled insanity'. The 'deliberate reversal of the facts' which extends even to the naming of its institutions, are 'deliber-ate exercises in *doublethink*', aimed to avert human equality (Part Two, ch. 9). Winston cannot perform his job without knowing that he is falsifying information. Yet he ought to believe, at the same time, that he is 'rectifying errors', and has to find the correct formula which will disguise, not reveal, the truth.

Part One, chapter 7 gives us Winston's intellectual history. He had begun to question the reasons why the Party falsifies the past some ten years before the novel begins. In 1965 purges eliminated all the original leaders of the revolution, except for Big Brother (rather as Stalin destroyed potential rivals). Three such men, Jones, Rutherford and Aaronson, were arrested, vanished for a year and then publicly confessed their crimes. Winston recalled seeing the three broken men in the Chestnut Tree Café. They were later rearrested and executed. In 1973, however, in the course of his work, Winston had discovered an old fragment of *The Times* which contained a photograph of the men in New York, on a date on which they had confessed to having been betraying state secrets in Eurasia. At the time Win-ston threw the paper down the memory hole, but now he reflects, somewhat naïvely, that 'It was enough to blow the Party to atoms, if in some way it could have been published to the world and its significance known.' The Party exerts its power by denying common-sense perceptions. Winston tries to fight the Party's infi-nite subjectivity by asserting his right to say '*that two plus two make four. If that is granted, all else follows.*'

In contrast to his co-workers in Minitrue, Winston alone values truth and exercises his memory (Part One, ch. 5). Syme and Parsons, orthodox Outer Party members, are savagely satiric bureaucratic types. Syme, who is working on the Newspeak dictionary, extols the 'beauty of the destruction of words' and endorses the Party's use of language to limit thought. At the moment, one can prevent thoughtcrime by self-discipline, or 'reality control', but, says Syme, by about 2050 all the literature of the past will have been destroyed (by being translated into pure Newspeak) and 'there will *be* no thought, as we understand it now. Orthodoxy means not thinking – not needing to think. Orthodoxy is unconsciousness.' When that day comes, double-think will no longer be required.

While Syme, who, Winston observes, is far too intelligent to escape punishment, represents the cold intellectual who enjoys manipulating ideas without regard for their human consequences (he looks forward to the extinction of all literature and culture), the fat and sweaty Parsons is the mediocrity best equipped to survive a regime which outlaws all independent thought; he is simply too stupid to have to practise doublethink.[66] When the telescreen announces a stream of false statistics, including a raise in the chocolate ration to twenty grams a week, Winston remembers that only yesterday the twenty-gram ration was announced as a reduction; Syme accepts the news, untroubled by the discrepancy, because he values orthodoxy above all; and Parsons rejoices, remarking that 'The Ministry of Plenty's certainly done a good job this year' because 'he could not follow the figures but he was aware that they were in some way a cause for satisfaction'. Syme lacks the 'saving stupidity' of Parsons, whose corruption is emotional or instinctual, rather than intellectual. Parsons completely accepts the will of the Party, even when he is accused by his seven-year-old daughter and arrested for 'thoughtcrime' (he has denounced Big Brother in his sleep). His sense of family loyalty is perverted by Party ideology.

Orwell's famous essay 'Politics and the English Language' is closely related to *Nineteen Eighty-Four*. Assuming that writing clearly demands an ethical choice, Orwell tried to demonstrate a link between effective writing and independent thinking, and gave examples of how orthodox opinions seemed to 'demand a lifeless, imitative style'. At worst, he said, observing a political speaker using familiar phrases, he had the feeling he was watching 'some kind of dummy', particularly when the light caught the speaker's glasses, so that they looked like blank discs (*CEJL*, 4.135). Winston has just this sensation when he observes the young man from the Fiction Department, who seems to be quack-quacking, each word 'pure orthodoxy, pure Ingsoc'. Orwell carries the figure of the Party ideologue to its satiric extreme in the rally in Victory Square at the climax of Hate Week, when the enemy abruptly switches from Eurasia to Eastasia (Part Two, ch. 9). The Hilteresque orator has 'boomed forth an endless catalogue of [Eurasian] atrocities, massacres, deportations, lootings, rapings, torture of civilians, lying propaganda, unjust aggressions, broken treaties', when he is handed the message that Eastasia is now the enemy. 'Nothing altered in his face or manner or in the content of what he was saying, but suddenly the names were different.' The vast audience absorbs the change, tears down the banners and posters (now in error, because of 'sabotage'), and the orator continues unabated.

Winston is stimulated to write in the diary by a glance he exchanges with O'Brien, the powerful, charismatic Inner Party member, which gives him hope that an opposition to the Party really exists. The possibility of an audience makes his writing political as well as personal. As he writes, his unfocused anger turns to hatred of Big Brother.

Winston's diary is not only an attempt to reclaim history, affirm ethical language, and communicate with a remote future audience; it is also therapy, enabling him to relive his past and expiate guilt and shame, as when he narrates the episode of his visit to a prostitute. Above all, in the dreams stimulated by the effort of writing, Winston retrieves the values of the past. Just as George Bowling makes a physical journey to find the 'Golden Country' of his boyhood, so Winston works on his dream-memories of his mother.[67] Vaguely aware that his mother in some way sacrificed herself for his survival, Winston learns to accept his guilt, because the memory has given him insight into normal human relationships. He now realises that her death

> had been tragic and sorrowful in a way that was no longer possible. Tragedy, he perceived, belonged to the ancient time, to a time when there were still privacy, love, and friendship, and when the members of a family stood by one another without needing to know the reason.

Today, 'there were fear, hatred, and pain, but no dignity of emotion, or deep or complex sorrow' (Part One, ch. 3).

When Winston first began to write, like Gordon Comstock he feels blocked by the thought that he has no audience, now or in the future. But, like Orwell in his essay 'Why I Write', he decides to write for posterity, 'the unborn'. The process of writing leads Winston to affirm its value, in spite of knowing that he is doomed and his writing will never be read: 'He was a lonely ghost uttering a truth that nobody would ever hear.' Writing itself has become a heroic means of 'staying sane', and 'carrying on the human heritage'.

Orwell's confusion of narrator with central character leads to a logical problem in the narrative. The narrator appears to be in charge of the story, and Winston's diary is printed in italics, set off from the text as are other 'documents'. Yet, if the narrator knows the entire story from the start, then he must be on the enemy side. In the first two parts of the novel, however, there are many indications that Winston and the narrator are one. Winston expresses Orwell's views, and makes cultural references inconsistent with his ahistorical education. In Part One, chapter 4 he mockingly compares his newly created comrade Ogilvy to Charlemagne and Julius Caesar. Despite the third-person narrative, the type-characters, and the satiric context of the political fable, the novel often sounds a note of personal appeal. When Winston writes his salutation in Part One, chapter 2, beginning, '*To the future or to the past, to a time when thought is free...*' we seem to be listening to Orwell's last will and testament. As in *The Road to Wigan Pier*, in this last novel Orwell did not separate self-revelation from his political theme.

JULIA AND THE PROLES: THE MORAL VALUE OF INSTINCT

Winston's memories of his marriage to the frigid Katharine (Part One, ch. 6), conditioned to believe the sex act a distasteful patriotic duty, reveal that, just as the Party controls members intellectually by forcing them to deny ordinary common sense, so it dominates them emotionally by forcing them to deny ordinary sexual feelings and family affection. Love and eroticism are private pleasures which threaten the Party's absolute control. Privacy itself is outlawed and all energies are channelled into communal activities. ('Ownlife' is pejorative Newspeak for the unhealthy desire to be alone.) The 'Appendix on Newspeak' explains that 'sexcrime' covers not only adultery and perversion, but any sexual act performed for pleasure, especially that between husband and wife, while 'goodsex' means chastity. The hate session shows how repressed sexuality becomes hysterical devotion to Big Brother and hatred of the enemy.

Even before he meets Julia, Winston reflects that 'the sexual act, successfully performed, was rebellion. Desire was thought-crime' (Part One, ch. 6). His affair with Julia in Part Two allows him to experience directly the sexual love and intimacy he has longed for. A complete departure from Orwell's previous hero-ines, Julia contrasts vividly with Winston in personality and attitude to the regime. Decisive, assertive, practical and sexually experienced, she initiates the affair and openly delights in outwit-ting the authorities. Her youth and physical and psychological toughness contrast with Winston's middle age, ill-health and fear-fulness. While Winston is an idealist, concerned about mankind's future as much as his own, Julia is a realist, eager to get what she can for herself. Much younger than Winston, she has no 'ancestral memory' that 'things had once been different'. Resourceful and willing to take risks, Julia arranges their rendez-vous, procures coffee and sugar, dares to buy lipstick, and dreams of owning a dress and high-heeled shoes.

Unlike Winston, who believes in the Brotherhood and dreams of overthrowing the regime, Julia accepts the idea that social change is impossible, and has learned to enjoy parts of life by circumventing the rules rather than by challenging them: 'any kind of organized revolt against the Party, which was bound to be a failure, struck her as stupid. The clever thing was to break the rules and stay alive all the same' (Part Two, ch. 3). Her philosophy is to yell with the crowd in public, and to seize any fleeting joy in private. When Winston remarks, 'We are the dead', anticipating their certain doom, Julia does not contradict him, but reminds him, 'We're not dead yet', and urges him to enjoy her beauty and her body while he can.

Julia is central to the novel and suitably occupies the middle section. She gives Winston hope, a reason to live, and strengthens his desire to rebel. Ironically, of course, she is also his downfall, and the old-fashioned room above Mr Charrington's shop, where they create a domestic idyll, turns out to be a trap. Julia reveals how thoroughly disoriented Winston is. He misinterprets her keen glances (she flings herself at his feet before he literally gets the message). At first he assumes she belongs to the Thought

Police, then to the Brotherhood. In contrast, he takes Mr Charrington for what he appears to be, and never suspects O'Brien's
overtures. Julia's attraction to Winston because she can tell he
is 'against *them*' also suggests that his 'facecrime' is visible to
others.

Julia shares Winston's hatred of the system, but expresses it
contemptuously, in language that startles him. Her open sensual-
ity and vulgar language seem 'natural and healthy' to the long-
repressed Winston. In one way Julia is the typical athletic girl
prefect, complete with school uniform and sash, not anti-intellectual but non-intellectual. When Winston reads aloud from *The
Book* she falls asleep. When he eagerly tells her about his discovery
that Aaronson, Rutherford and Jones had falsely incriminated
themselves, she is unimpressed. 'In some ways she was far more
acute than Winston, and far less susceptible to Party propaganda', anticipating what he will read in *The Book* when she
suggests that the war is a complete myth (Part Two, ch. 3).
Following her hedonistic code, Julia arrives at Winston's political
insight by a simpler route.

Amoral, self-indulgent, hostile to other women (she lives in
a building that 'stinks' of women), vain and sensual, uneducated
(only indoctrinated by the Party), unable to carry on an abstract
discussion, Julia might seem a negative stereotype, unless we
see these characteristics in the context of the novel. Like Winston,
Julia is a symbolic figure, and their scenes together are strongly
influenced by D. H. Lawrence. One critic has pointed out many
parallels between *Lady Chatterley's Lover* and *Nineteen Eighty-Four*,
and notes that, although Lawrence's novel attacks the obsession
with money and consequent devaluation of sexual instincts, 'the
life-denying Party ethos of *Nineteen Eighty-Four* merely codifies
and rationalises the puritanism pilloried by Lawrence. Both
books are distress-signals warning of the imminent shipwreck
of all personal intimacy.'[68]

In their first sexual encounter Winston is hesitant and shy,
but when Julia assures him that she is completely promiscuous
and 'corrupt', and positively enjoys sex for its own sake, he is
both sexually and politically aroused. It was 'above all what
he wanted to hear. Not merely the love of one person, but the
animal instinct, the simple undifferentiated desire: that was the
force that would tear the Party to pieces' (Part Two, ch. 2).
Julia's affairs, like Winston's writing, are political acts, and Win-

ston's love-affair encourages his intellectual self-assertion. Orwell follows Lawrence in opposing the corruptibility of the intellect to the fidelity of animal instincts (what Lawrence calls 'blood-consciousness').

Like Lawrence, Orwell opposes the instinctive sexual impulse to the artificial, dehumanising political and economic system. As in *Lady Chatterley's Lover*, the lovers seek refuge in a natural setting, among trees and bluebells. Orwell suggests an analogy between Winston's writing and the thrush's song when Winston wonders, 'What made it sit at the edge of the lonely wood and pour its music into nothingness?' (Part Two, ch. 2). The bird's instinct to sing, Winston's desire to write and to love, are aspects of the natural drive towards individual fulfilment the Party suppresses.

Winston's sexual love for Julia modulates into 'deep tenderness', and comes to symbolise the continuity of love passed on from generation to generation despite the Party. When she brings chocolate to their first meeting, the smell of it stirs a 'painful and troubling memory' in Winston (Part Two, ch. 2). Later, in bed with Julia, he wakes and remembers that the day he stole the family's chocolate ration and ran out of the house with it was the day his mother and sister disappeared; ever since then he has been haunted by guilt (Part Two, ch. 7). Julia's gift of chocolate connects her with his lost mother's love. By enabling him to retrieve his guilt for his mother's death, she helps him distinguish real emotions from those induced by the Party's thought-control. Indeed, even at the end of the novel, after Winston has betrayed Julia, O'Brien does not succeed in eradicating the memory of his mother's love. Despite its consequences, the affair with Julia symbolises the continuity of human love.

The 'simple, undifferentiated desire', the sexual drive which animates Julia despite her regimented upbringing, links her to the proles, the vast swarming underclass of Oceania, who live to work, drink, gamble and reproduce. 'Proletarian' derives from the Latin *proles* or 'offspring', and originally designated the lowest class, which serves the state only by breeding. Marx used the word 'proletariat' to define the industrial working class, and urged this class to seize power in a 'dictatorship of the proletariat'. Orwell's use of 'prole' defines them in a manner closer to the earlier meaning of the word, and exposes the Marxist ideal as a totalitarian myth. Though surrounded by posters of noblebrowed prole soldiers and workers, Party members despise them (Syme remarks that 'proles are not human beings').

In contrast to the Party members' indifference to suffering, the proles' instinctive fellow-feeling has not been corrupted. In the first chapter of the novel Winston records in his diary a visit to the cinema. When a prole woman protests that a newsreel revealing women and children being killed should not be shown in front of children, she is hustled out by police and Winston calls her complaint a 'typical prole reaction'. In the conversation in the canteen Syme expresses perverse delight in public hangings (Part One, ch. 5); and later on, after a rocket-bomb attack in a prole district, Winston kicks aside a severed human hand (Part One, ch. 8), hardly aware of what he is doing.

This happens on his way to the pub where he hopes to talk to prole survivors of the pre-revolutionary period, to see if they can tell him what life was really like before the war. Though his visit is disappointing, it does not kill his belief that 'if there is any hope, it lies in the proles'. As he almost lets slip in conversation with Syme, Winston believes that, since the proles are outside the Party, uneducated in doublethink or Newspeak, they are not corrupted, like Syme, Parsons and himself. In prison Winston especially notes the difference between proles and Party members. While common criminals show contempt for the guards, the political prisoners, implicated by ideology in their own punishment, are silent, cowed with terror.

Winston's love for Julia enables him to see the proles as fully human. The prole woman singing as she hangs out her washing strikes him as beautiful because she represents the nurturing maternity that he lost when his mother disappeared. He concludes that people of two generations ago 'were governed by private loyalties', as his mother had been, and that 'the proles had remained in this condition. They were not loyal to a party or a country or an idea, they were loyal to one another', and 'had held on to primitive emotions which he himself had to relearn with conscious effort'. He guiltily recalls the severed hand he had kicked aside in the street. Contradicting Syme, he tells Julia, 'The proles are human beings .... . We are not human' (Part Two, ch. 7).

O'BRIEN AND THE MYSTIQUE OF POWER

If the proles are the most ignorant and decent people in the novel, O'Brien is the most knowledgeable and the most evil. 'Tormentor, ... protector, ... inquisitor, ... friend' (Part Two, ch. 2), he has orchestrated Winston's surveillance for seven years, and now supervises his re-education. O'Brien is the completely corrupt intellectual. As the part-author of Goldstein's *Book*, he has mastered all the political and social arguments against the Party, but dispenses with truth and morality for the sake of power. When Winston sees O'Brien enter the prison cell, he exclaims, 'They've got you too!' 'They got me a long time ago' – is the ironic reply. In the last section of the novel – in scenes inspired partly by Dostoevsky's 'Grand Inquisitor' chapters of *The Brothers Karamazov*, and partly by contemporary reports of Stalin's purges – Winston and O'Brien engage in an unequal duel. O'Brien's absolute physical power enables him to force Winston to accept his essentially mad belief in a society based on the principle of power.

Early in the novel, Winston realises that the government manipulates the past to control the present, but wonders what its ultimate motive can be. Later, he breaks off reading Goldstein's *Book* at a similar question: why do men seek absolute power? We know from his disagreement with Burnham that Orwell did not believe that human conduct was ruled by power-hunger. The answer the novel seems to offer is that sadistic enjoyment of power predominates at various times and places in history. Orwell's polemical strategy is to imagine how total terror, the opposite to his ideal of democratic socialism, could dominate forever.

Like Dostoevsky's Grand Inquisitor, O'Brien believes men incapable and unworthy of free choice. Winston argues that all men are potentially good, O'Brien the opposite. But O'Brien goes one step further: the essential difference between this terror and the terrors of the past, he says, is that modern systems have the technological means to be absolute. 'One must not make martyrs', he says, underlining the regime's intention to break its victims' spirits, not just kill them. In such a situation, as Winston realises, there is no escape and no possibility of heroism. O'Brien boasts he will 'cure' Winston, make him 'perfect', or perfectly willing to agree that $2 + 2 = 5$. He boasts that the

Party has transformed the basic principles of social life, for 'no-one dares trust a wife or a child or a friend any longer'. He looks forward to the future, when 'the sex-instinct will be eradicated and there will be no loyalty, except loyalty toward the Party...no love, except the love of Big Brother'. There will be no science, literature, art, no pleasure save the sadistic 'thrill of victory'. O'Brien's image of the future is 'a boot stamping on a human face – forever'.

Orwell created Winston's state of mind and the perverse intimacy of torturer and victim by intensifying the prep-school memories of his essay 'Such, Such Were the Joys'. Orwell recalled the pain of separation from his parents, feelings of guilt and rejection, shame about his body, assumption that he was a worthless failure; cold, hunger and discomfort; indoctrination in the ways of a rigidly hierarchical society. He remembered being watched, imagining that 'Sambo', the headmaster, had an army of spies who would report his illicit visits to the sweetshop. Like the young Eric Blair, Winston has no privacy, no close friendships, he lives in a 'locked loneliness' where a stray glance from O'Brien is a significant event. O'Brien is compared to 'a schoolmaster questioning a promising pupil' and making him suffer (Part Three, ch. 3). In the essay Orwell remembers with horror his hypocritical desire to 'suck up' to the tyrannical 'Flip'; in the novel Winston hero-worships O'Brien. Even under torture Winston longs for his approval, clings to him like a baby, looks at him gratefully when the pain stops, and feels that 'in some sense that went deeper than friendship, they were intimates' (Part Three, ch. 2). Like Winston in Oceania, Orwell at St Cyprian's experienced 'a sense of desolate loneliness and helplessness, of being locked up...in a world of good and evil where the rules were such that it was actually not possible for me to keep them' (*CEJL*, IV.334).[69] Both places are ruled by a capricious power, rather than by a written code of law, and in both the central character is torn between his desire to rebel against the abuse of power and his desperate longing to be part of a community.

Most critics of Orwell would agree with George Woodcock that *Nineteen Eighty-Four* is 'an uneasy combination of several kinds of fiction'.[70] Readers have particularly objected to what seems the gratuitous sadistic cruelty of the last part. Winston's suffering obliterates the novel's earlier satiric wit, emphasises his cowardice and betrayal, and seems to suggest that the socialist ideal of brotherhood will always be defeated. The problem with the novel is not only its imperfect mixture of styles, but also that Orwell breaks the conventions of both dominant forms, realism and utopian romance, and the reader's expectations are disappointed. At Winston's lowest point we expect some twist that will set him free, some lightening of the plot, or at least some enlightenment as to what all this repression and torture is *for*. Although a faint flicker of Orwellian humour survives in the last chapter, where we learn that Winston has to attend bi-weekly committee meetings on some obscure points of the eleventh edition of the Newspeak dictionary (a different kind of torture), the end of the novel is totally bleak. Not only is Winston neither rescued nor rewarded; he is also reduced to infantilism, cowardice and self-pitying alcoholism. His enlightenment about the meaning of his life – that he is merely subject to the monstrous lust for power of those like O'Brien – coincides with the extinction of all hope.

Orwell's novel does not belong to that category of art which offers consolation. It reveals his acute historical sense, his imaginative sympathy with the millions of those persecuted and murdered in the name of the absolutist ideologies of the twentieth century. Orwell's depiction of the absurd, squalid and cruel life of an Everyman, trapped in a bureaucratised world where independent action and heroism are impossible, makes *Nineteen Eighty-Four* closer in spirit to Franz Kafka's fables or to Alexander Solzhenitsyn's tales of the Soviet prison camps than to other English novels.

Leftist critics like Isaac Deutscher have argued that the book has served only to heighten Western fear and hatred of Communism, because Orwell depicts totalitarian society as 'ruled by a disembodied sadism', and replaces political analysis with a 'mysticism of cruelty'.[71] But the sado-masochistic relationship between Winston and O'Brien shows, as Denis Donoghue has argued, 'the character and force of a system; its appalling capacity to operate independently of the people who compose it'.[72] *Nineteen Eighty-Four* succeeds brilliantly as a political fable. As Anthony Burgess writes, it is 'one of the few dystopian visions to have changed men's habits of thought. It is possible to say that the ghastly future Orwell foretells will not come about, simply because he has foretold it: we have been warned.'[73]

9

Conclusion

Although Orwell's innovative work in diverse genres and his unusual choice of literary subjects provided important models, his influence on contemporary literature and thought has been primarily as a moralist. His sceptical, serious, mocking and irascible 'radical Tory' attitude was a major influence on the poets and novelists of the 1940s and 1950s. His non-fiction books and journalism raised the level of travel writing and other kinds of analytic discourse, and *Nineteen Eighty-Four* added a new and serious element to science fiction. It not only warned of the dangers to freedom posed by totalitarian tendencies in East and West, but provided a language to describe it.

Orwell's early novels, essays and documentaries influenced the poets and novelists of the 'Movement' in the 1950s, and the sociological critics, journalists and essayists of the 1960s. In his introduction to *New Lines* (1956), an anthology of the Movement poets (including Kingsley Amis, Donald Davie, Philip Larkin and John Wain), Robert Conquest defined their empirical attitude to experience and their 'reverence for the real person or event' as 'part of the general intellectual ambience of our time'. He named Orwell 'with his principle of real, rather than ideological, honesty' as 'one of the major influences on modern poetry', and detected Orwell's traditional spirit in the poets' 'refusal to abandon a rational structure and comprehensible language'.[74] Like Orwell, these poets emphasise prosaic, everyday experience, rather than the convoluted mysticism of the later T. S. Eliot. A good example from the anthology is Larkin's famous poem 'Church Going'. Like *A Clergyman's Daughter* and Orwell's review of Muggeridge's *The Thirties*, the poem accepts the abandonment of religious beliefs but mourns the cultural loss this entails. Like Orwell, Larkin respects the traditional way of life the church represents, even though he feels cut off from it:

> though I've no idea
> What this accoutred frowsty barn is worth,
> It pleases me to stand in silence here.

And he concludes that the church is after all 'A serious house on serious earth' whose function 'never can be obsolete'.[75] The Movement writers began by sharing Orwell's socialist sympathies, but Amis and Larkin especially became increasingly conservative, intensifying their nostalgia for the past and their dislike of modern life.

Mary McCarthy regarded Orwell's reluctance to abandon his early values as admirable in the man, but a limitation in his thinking. In her view, 'The longing to go back to some simpler form of life, to be rid of modern so-called conveniences, is typical of a whole generation of middle-class radicals (myself included) whose loudest spokesman was Orwell.'[76] This half-conservative, half-iconoclastic attitude was a major influence on the 'Angry Young Men' of the 1950s. Charles, the hero of John Wain's *Hurry On Down* (1953), is a lonely Gordon Comstock character with an Oxford education but no decent prospects, who suffers humiliation in his pursuit of a girl. Wain's autobiography, *Sprightly Running* (1962), sounds the Orwellian themes of the sense of belonging to an embattled middle class in the 'age of the roughs', and regret for the 'dwindling countryside'.

Donald Davie has described the Movement as 'the first concerted though unplanned invasion of the literary Establishment by the scholarship-boys of the petty bourgeoisie'.[77] Kingsley Amis identified with Orwell's lower-middle-class heroes and their obsession with class in his *Lucky Jim* (1953), which places the comically awkward hero in the context of the red-brick university of the 1950s. Jim competes for the girl with a caricature 'pansy' of the type so detested by Orwell. Amis's satiric targets, like Orwell's, are pretension, snobbery and flashy modernity. This attitude has persisted throughout Amis's long career. In his recent novel *Difficulties with Girls* (1988), the hero mocks the local pub's smart new partitions, carpets and suburban atmosphere.

Another recent incarnation of the Orwell hero appears in William Boyd's *A Good Man in Africa* (1981), whose hero, Morgan Leafy, is a comic version of Orwell's Flory: overweight, alcoholic and depressive, pursuing a girl in a steamy, inhospitable and snobbish post-colonial society. The good man of the title is a

Scot called Murray, whose death provides the Orwellian tragi-comic ending. (William Boyd has also written a screenplay, *Good and Bad at Games*, filmed for television in 1985, which takes up the 1930s theme of public-school brutality.)

Orwell's essays and reportage, which revived a nineteenth-century tradition of investigation and exposure of social injustice, have had a beneficial influence on contemporary non-fiction writers and journalists. Orwell's autobiographical method, collo-quial speaking voice and eye for concrete detail provided a form for James Baldwin's essays, the travel books of Mary McCarthy and Norman Lewis, and the political reportage of Norman Mailer and Joan Didion. Orwell also inspired Richard Hoggart's influen-tial study of class and culture in post-war Britain, *The Uses of Literacy* (1957). More than anyone else, Orwell forced social com-mentators to articulate a moral point of view, and thus enabled these non-fiction forms to flourish in ways the self-conscious modern novel has not.

After his untimely death, the critics tended to canonise Orwell. In an influential obituary V. S. Pritchett called him 'the wintry conscience' of the 1930s generation that had espoused leftist political ideas, and cited his independence and stubborn lack of illusion.[78] In his persuasive introduction to the first American edition of *Homage to Catalonia* (1952), Lionel Trilling praised the book as a 'genuine moral triumph' and defined Orwell as a 'figure', not a genius, a man who 'communicates to us the sense that what he has done any one of us could do' – had we the honesty and fearlessness to do so.[79]

This identification of Orwell's personal virtue with the value of his ideas inevitably contributed to the backlash from the Left, who blamed his novel for fostering hysterical anti-Communist hatred during the Cold War. In the 1960s and 1970s the Marxist critics Isaac Deutscher and Raymond Williams accused Orwell of being revisionist, reactionary and cynical about the working class. And Mary McCarthy's review of Orwell's *Collected Essays, Journalism and Letters* in 1969 called him a failure as a political thinker, and blamed him for the right-wing views of 'his main progeny', Kingsley Amis, Bernard Levin and John Osborne.

Animal Farm and *Nineteen Eighty-Four* have remained consis-tently popular, however, and have played their part in the recent relaxation of ideological repression in Eastern Europe. Trans-lated into more than sixty languages, they circulated for years in clandestine editions behind the Iron Curtain. The Polish dissident writer Czeslaw Milosz has recorded in *The Captive Mind* (1953) that, although Orwell's satires were 'difficult to obtain and dangerous to possess' and therefore known only to a handful of Inner Party members, these readers were fascinated by the allegory, which violated 'the prescription of socialist realism and the demands of the censor'. Even those who had only heard of, but had not read, Orwell were 'amazed that a writer who never lived in Russia should have so keen a perception into its life'.[80] These novels have had wider circulation in film versions: *Animal Farm* was made into a cartoon film in 1954 (unfortunately with a happy ending, which destroyed much of its point); *Nineteen Eighty-Four* was filmed twice, in 1956 and 1984, and has been dramatised for television.

Orwell is a great rejuvenator of genres. *Nineteen Eighty-Four* rescued the futuristic novel from the sub-literature of science fiction and made it intellectually respectable. Ray Bradbury's *Fahrenheit 451* (1954) and Anthony Burgess's *A Clockwork Orange* (1962) were both influenced by Orwell, and both were made into effective films. Bradbury's novel takes up Orwell's theme of repression by the destruction of culture, and his hero, Montag, is employed to destroy books, as Winston is employed to destroy the factual record. The novel imagines a dissident community where people memorise great literary works so that they can attempt to pass on 'the human heritage'.

Anthony Burgess extends Orwell's question about why men seek power and discusses the problem of evil itself. *A Clockwork Orange* is a satiric fable set, like Orwell's novel, in a not-so-distant future England, a work-state where teenage criminals roam free at night, and where political expediency has replaced the rule of law and ethical code. The protagonist–narrator Alex, a sociopathic delinquent, delights, like Orwell's O'Brien, in the idea of grinding his boot into human faces. Alex is arrested and his sadistic desires are cruelly inhibited by behavioural conditioning and drugs, a process the government considers more efficient than traditional methods of punishment. But the treatment offers Alex no chance to repent or atone for his crimes, and deprives him of his ability to choose good or evil. He becomes a robot-like creature, whose wickedness is merely overlaid by superficial conditioning. Once the conditioning is reversed, he reverts to his previous sadistic fantasies. Burgess shows that repressive, totali-

tarian methods are no more successful at eradicating the evil
in man than they are at destroying the good. Man is an infinitely
more complex creature than crude modern political theories
would have us believe. The novel's outstanding Orwellian feature
is the vicious invented language in which Alex tells his story.
A mixture of Russian vocabulary and gypsy and cockney slang,
it expresses his anti-social hatred as powerfully as the actions
he describes. Like Newspeak, it articulates the moral atmosphere
of the novel's imaginary world.

The brilliant vocabulary of the self-justifying abuse of power
in *Nineteen Eighty-Four* has had a pervasive influence on our
general culture. Like Shakespeare and Kipling, Orwell has added
to our stock of proverbial, ironic and apt expressions. The Russian
invasion of Hungary in 1956, and of Czechoslovakia in 1968,
and the publication in the West of the experiences of those persecuted have made the novel seem much less a piece of sadistic
science fiction than a work of compassionate realism. 'Unperson',
'some are more equal than others', 'doublethink', 'memory hole',
'Newspeak', 'thoughtcrime' – these terms are now indispensable,
whether to describe the convolutions of Marxist policies or the
contradictions of the American war in Vietnam.

Denis Donoghue has defined Orwell's special contribution to
the traditional political fable as the 'representation of systematic
cruelty and intimidation by analogy with the deliberate degradation of language'.[81] After reading documentary evidence about
totalitarian repression and visiting Czechoslovakia, Tom Stoppard wrote two plays which use Orwell's analogy to poignant
effect. *Every Good Boy Deserves Favour* (1978) is set in a Soviet
psychiatric hospital, where a dissident, Alexander Panov, is being
punished. An orchestra accompanies the action, and the play's
central metaphor is the conflict between the 'orchestration' of
society and the discordant note represented by Panov. When
Alexander maintains, 'I have no symptoms, I have opinions',
the doctor replies, 'Your opinions are your symptoms. Your disease is dissent.'[82] Alexander sings a song with an Orwellian echo
to his small son Sacha:

> Dear Sacha, try to see
> what they call their liberty
> is just the freedom to agree
> that one and one is sometimes three.

Sacha urges him to get out of the hospital by agreeing with the doctor:

Sacha: Be brave and tell them lies!
Alex: How can that be right?
Sacha: If they're wicked how can it be wrong?
Alex: It helps them to go on being wicked. It helps people to think that perhaps they're not so wicked after all.[83]

Stoppard's hero, like Winston Smith, clings obstinately to the distinction between right and wrong, truth and lies, despite the doctors' abuse of language and attempt to disorient him with drugs.

Stoppard's *Professional Foul* (1978), a play for television, also concerns the rights of the individual versus the rights of the state. The play is structured on the conjunction of a World Cup football match and a philosophy congress, both held in Prague, and focuses on the conflict between the views of Anderson, an English philosophy don, and Pavel Hollar, an ex-philosophy-teacher and ex-pupil of Anderson in England, now reduced to working as a cleaner as punishment for political dissent. Anderson's philosophy is an elaborate linguistic game, which enables him at first to escape the moral responsibility to help Hollar smuggle his thesis out of the country. He believes that, because ethics are subjective, human creations, individual rights are subject to the consent of the group, or the state. But Hollar's experience of state 'correctness', and his willingness to endure persecution because he has something to say persuade Anderson that free speech has value in itself and that his own subjectivity is immoral. When he addresses the congress Anderson unfashionably maintains, 'There is a sense of right and wrong which precedes utterance', and the moderator interrupts this dangerous speech with a fake fire alarm.[84] In Stoppard's play children function as moral arbiters, as Orwell's proles do in *Nineteen Eighty-Four*. Chetwyn, another participant in the congress (who has come with the intention of helping Czech dissidents), says that complex moral questions should always be tried out on 'men much less clever than us', and that in these cases he usually consults his eight year-old son.[85] Like *Nineteen Eighty-Four*, the play attacks intellectuals for their hypocrisy and collusion with repression. The subject of Anderson's speech, the problem of an ethics divorced from

religious belief, and his conclusion, that we cannot do without
traditional ethics, bring us back to the theme of *A Clergyman's
Daughter*, but Stoppard's use of the drama for political and moral
debate shows his link to the later Orwell.

V. S. Naipaul, one of our most eminent living novelists, has
praised Orwell's courage in breaking away from conventional
forms and subjects, in stripping 'himself of all his earliest assumptions', and has called him 'the most imaginative man in English
history [because] he travelled in a new direction'.[86] For Naipaul,
the novelist of unstable, brutal societies, Orwell's greatest
achievement lies in his refusal to write in the fixed form of the
English social novel, in his ability to record and interpret the
political and social changes of his time.

Notes

1. W. H. Auden, 'Honour', in *The Old School*, ed. Graham Greene (London: Jonathan Cape, 1934), p. 17.
2. Evelyn Waugh, *A Little Learning* (London: Sidgwick and Jackson, 1964), p. 108.
3. Anthony Powell, 'Wat'ry Glade', in *The Old School*, p. 152.
4. Cyril Connolly, *Enemies of Promise* (London: Routledge and Kegan Paul, 1938), p. 198.
5. *Orwell Remembered*, ed. Audrey Coppard and Bernard Crick (London: BBC, Ariel Books, 1984), p. 53.
6. Ibid., p. 116.
7. Orwell was not alone in questioning the public-school code. Beginning with Alec Waugh's *The Loom of Youth* (1917) the public schools were attacked for the next two decades.
8. *Orwell Remembered*, pp. 68–75.
9. Victor Gollancz, Foreword to *The Road to Wigan Pier*; reprinted in *George Orwell: The Critical Heritage*, ed. Jeffrey Meyers (London: Routledge and Kegan Paul, 1975), p. 95.
10. *The Critical Heritage*, p. 144.
11. *Orwell Remembered*, p. 171.
12. Anthony Powell, *To Keep the Ball Rolling* (Harmondsworth, Middlesex: Penguin, 1983), p. 336.
13. *Orwell Remembered*, p. 169.
14. Ibid., p. 184.
15. Ibid., p. 202.
16. Q. D. Leavis, 'The Literary Life Respectable', *Scrutiny*, 9 (1940), 173–176; reprinted in *George Orwell: The Critical Heritage*, p. 189.
17. John Wain, 'The Last of George Orwell', *Twentieth Century*, 155 (January 1954), 71–78; reprinted in *George Orwell: The Critical Heritage*, p. 326.
18. George Woodcock, *The Crystal Spirit*, revised edition (London: Fourth Estate, 1984), p. ix.
19. Raymond Williams, *George Orwell* (New York: Viking, 1971), p. 48.
20. See Samuel Hynes, *The Auden Generation* (New York: Viking, 1976), pp. 209, 228.
21. Julian Symons, *The Thirties: A Dream Revolved* (London: Faber and Faber, 1960), p. 174.
22. Rudyard Kipling, *Something of Myself* (London: Macmillan, 1937), p. 155.
23. Ibid., p. 207.

24. The poem is 'Love on a Farm'.
25. D. H. Lawrence, 'John Galsworthy', in *D. H. Lawrence: Selected Literary Criticism*, ed. Anthony Beal (New York: Viking, 1966), p. 118.
26. David Lodge, *The Writer at the Crossroads* (Ithaca, New York: Cornell University Press, 1971), p. 219.
27. Joyce Cary's *The African Witch* (1936), set in Nigeria, borrows similar features from *A Passage to India* and has many elements in common with *Burmese Days*.
28. Jeffrey Meyers has suggested that U Po Kyin is based on the Malay chieftain Doramin, in Joseph Conrad's *Lord Jim* (1900), who is so fat that he cannot move without help, and confides in his wife. See *A Reader's Guide to George Orwell* (London: Thames and Hudson, 1975), p. 167. Clearly Kyin is a figure derived from literature, not life.

    The influence of *Lord Jim* is also apparent in Veraswamy's emphatic reference to Kyin as having 'the cunning of the crocodile'. In chapter 23 of *Lord Jim* the master of the ship taking Jim to Batu Kring talks of a false Malay with the '"weapons of a crocodile"'.
29. Orwell probably derived the idea of Ma Hla May's accusation in church from D. H. Lawrence's 'Fanny and Annie', where a young man who is about to marry is denounced in church by the mother of a pregnant girl.
30. Jeffrey Meyers has suggested that Orwell named Verrall jokingly after Dr A. W. Verrall, editor of Greek and Latin textbooks (*Reader's Guide*, p. 167 n. 8). It seems more likely, however, that he took the name from Wells's *In the Days of the Comet*, where Verrall is the rich cad who elopes with the hero's girl.
31. Evelyn Waugh, *Put Out More Flags* (Boston, Massachusetts: Little, Brown, 1942), p. 235.
32. Richard Hoggart, 'Introduction to *The Road to Wigan Pier*', in *George Orwell: A Collection of Critical Essays*, ed. Raymond Williams (Englewood Cliffs, New Jersey: Prentice-Hall, 1974), p. 38.
33. See Bernard Crick, *George Orwell* (Boston, Massachusetts: Little, Brown, 1980), pp. 87–88.
34. In chapter 3 Flory says of the British, 'they build a prison and call it progress', and regrets that Veraswamy does not recognise the allusion. He echoes a British chieftain whom Tacitus quotes as saying (of the Romans) 'they make a desert and call it peace' (*Agricola*, 30). The emphasis on prison would be more likely to occur to a policeman than to a timber merchant.
35. In a letter of February 1934 to his agent, in response to criticism of the last two or three pages of *Burmese Days*, Orwell remarked, 'I hate a novel in which the principal characters are not disposed of at the end' (*CEJL*, 1.134).
36. Orwell used this couplet from a familiar hymn as the epigraph for the novel.
37. Orwell gives the opportunistic politician names associative of hypocrisy and snobbery: Blifil, the unctuous clergyman of Fielding's *Tom Jones*, and Gordon, like his own name, Blair, a Scottish name. Orwell associated such names with the pretentious cult of Scotland.
38. Keith Alldritt, *The Making of George Orwell* (London: Edward Arnold, 1969),

p. 29; Jenni Calder, *Chronicles of Conscience: A Study of George Orwell and Arthur Koestler* (London: Secker and Warburg, 1968), p. 90.

39. See his review of Malcolm Muggeridge's *The Thirties* (*CEJL*, 2.15).
40. Dorothy's attitude to Warburton is very like Alvina's to her suitor Dr Mitchell in D. H. Lawrence's *The Lost Girl*: viewed close up he is hairy, coarse and repellent.
41. An allusion to the well-known Latin funerary inscription 'Et in Arcadia ego' ('And I too lived in Arcadia').
42. Orwell probably based Mr Tallboys on the Reverend Harold Davidson, the Rector of Stiffkey, in Norfolk, who created a scandal and was defrocked in 1932. For years he preached his Sunday sermon in Norfolk and then spent the rest of the week in London, where he pursued young women in order to 'save' them. See Ronald Blythe, *The Age of Illusion* (Harmondsworth, Middlesex: Penguin, 1964), pp. 156–178.
43. *Orwell Remembered*, pp. 100–101.
44. Alldritt, *The Making of George Orwell*, p. 31, discusses the Joycean influences.
45. Wells, *The History of Mr Polly*, ch. 7.
46. The shanty begins,

> Here a sheer hulk, lies poor Tom Bowling,
> The darling of our crew;
> No more he'll hear the tempest howling,
> For death has brought him to.
> His form was of the manliest beauty,
> His heart was kind and soft:
> Faithful below he did his duty,
> And now he's gone aloft.

47. Hynes, *The Auden Generation*, p. 373.
48. Isaac Rosenfeld, 'Decency and Death', *Partisan Review*, 17 (May 1950); reprinted in *George Orwell: The Critical Heritage*, p. 172.
49. *Orwell: The Lost Writings*, ed. W. J. West (New York: Arbor House, 1985), p. 61. (Published in Great Britain as *Orwell: The War Broadcasts*.)
50. E. M. Forster, 'A Note on the Way' (1934), in *Abinger Harvest* (New York: Meridian, 1955), p. 72.
51. Thomas More, *Utopia* (New York: Appleton-Century-Crofts, 1949), p. 26.
52. *Orwell: The Lost Writings*, p. 112.
53. See Jeffrey Meyers, *A Reader's Guide to George Orwell*, pp. 130–143.
54. Woodcock, *The Crystal Spirit*, p. ix.
55. See Paul Johnson, *Modern Times* (New York: Harper and Row, 1985), p. 263.
56. Stephen Greenblatt, 'Orwell as Satirist', in *George Orwell: A Collection of Critical Essays*, p. 108.
57. See *Richard III*, ii.ii.28. Richard, like Stalin, puts his unsuspecting, innocent victims to death.
58. *British Pamphleteers*, vol. 1 (London: Allan Wingate, 1948), Introduction by Orwell, p. 10.

59. In *George Orwell: The Critical Heritage*, p. 20.

60. Ibid., p. 200.

61. Ibid., p. 208.

62. Alldritt, *The Making of George Orwell*, p. 151.

63. Fredric Warburg, publisher's report, in *George Orwell: The Critical Heritage*, p. 248.

64. See, for example, the memoirs of two stubborn survivors of totalitarian repression: Nadezhda Mandelstam, *Hope Against Hope* (New York: Atheneum, 1970), and Nien Cheng, *Life and Death in Shanghai* (New York: Grove, 1986).

65. See his essay 'Revenge is Sour' in *CEJL*, 4.3–6.

66. Parsons surely owes his physical character to the Parsons in Wells's *Mr Polly*: 'of an ampler build, already promising fatness, with curly hair and a lot of rolling, rollicking, curly features, and a large, blob-shaped nose' (Part One, ch. 3).

67. Orwell probably drew on Stephen Dedalus's vision of his mother, 'beastly dead', and his shame connected with his behaviour towards her, in the 'nighttown' chapter of *Ulysses*.

68. Michael L. Ross, '"Carrying on the Human Heritage": From *Lady Chatterley's Lover* to *Nineteen Eighty-Four*', *D. H. Lawrence Review*, 17 (Spring 1984), 7–8.

69. As so often in Orwell, his experience seems to have been filtered through his reading of Wells. In chapter 1 of *The History of Mr Polly*, Mr Polly thinks of 'the Divinity as of a limitless Being having the nature of a schoolmaster and making infinite rules, known and unknown, rules that were always ruthlessly enforced, and with an infinite capacity for punishment, and, most horrible of all to think of, limitless powers of espial'.

70. Woodcock, *The Crystal Spirit*, p. x.

71. Isaac Deutscher, '*1984* – The Mysticism of Cruelty', in *Russia in Transition and Other Essays* (New York: Coward-McCann 1960), pp. 250–265; reprinted in *George Orwell: A Collection of Critical Essays*, pp. 130–131.

72. Denis Donoghue, '*Nineteen Eighty-Four*: Politics and Fable', in *George Orwell and 'Nineteen Eighty-Four'*, ed. John Broderick (Washington, DC: Library of Congress, 1984), p. 69.

73. Anthony Burgess, *The Novel Now* (New York: Pegasus, 1970), p. 43.

74. Robert Conquest (ed.), *New Lines* (London: Macmillan, 1956), p. xv.

75. Ibid., p. 21.

76. Mary McCarthy, 'The Writing on the Wall', *New York Review of Books*, (30 January 1969), 3–6; reprinted in *The Writing on the Wall* (Harmondsworth, Middlesex: Penguin, 1973), p. 165.

77. Donald Davie, 'My Cambridge', in *My Oxford, My Cambridge*, ed. Ann Thwaite and Ronald Hayman (New York: Taplinger, 1979), p. 301.

78. V. S. Pritchett, 'George Orwell', *New Statesman*, 39 (28 January 1950), 96; reprinted in *George Orwell: The Critical Heritage*, p. 294.

79. Lionel Trilling, 'George Orwell and the Politics of Truth', *The Opposing Self* (New York: Viking, 1955), pp. 153, 157.

80. Czeslaw Milosz, *The Captive Mind* (New York: Knopf, 1953); reprinted in *George Orwell: The Critical Heritage*, p. 286.

81. Donoghue, in *George Orwell and 'Nineteen Eighty-Four'*, p. 66.

82. Tom Stoppard, *Every Good Boy Deserves Favour* (New York: Random House, 1978), p. 30.
83. Ibid., pp. 34–35.
84. Tom Stoppard, *Professional Foul* (New York: Random House, 1978), p. 90.
85. Ibid., p. 79.
86. Bharati Mukherjee and Robert Boyers, 'A Conversation with V. S. Naipaul', *Salmagundi*, 54 (Fall 1981), 11.

Select Bibliography

Place of publication is London, unless otherwise indicated.

ORWELL'S PRINCIPAL WRITINGS

Down and Out in Paris and London (Victor Gollancz, 1933)
Burmese Days (New York: Harper, 1934)
A Clergyman's Daughter (Victor Gollancz, 1935)
Keep the Aspidistra Flying (Victor Gollancz, 1936)
The Road to Wigan Pier (Victor Gollancz, 1937)
Homage to Catalonia (Secker and Warburg, 1938)
Coming Up for Air (Victor Gollancz, 1939)
Animal Farm (Secker and Warburg, 1945)
Nineteen Eighty-Four (Secker and Warburg, 1949)
Collected Essays, Journalism and Letters, ed. Sonia Orwell and Ian Angus 4 vols (Secker and Warburg, 1968)
Nineteen Eighty-Four Facsimile, ed. Peter Davidson (Secker and Warburg, 1984)
Orwell: The War Commentaries, ed. W. J. West (New York: Pantheon, 1985)
Orwell: The Lost Writings, ed. W. J. West (New York: Arbor House, 1985)

SELECTED CRITICISM

Keith Alldritt, *The Making of George Orwell* (Edward Arnold, 1969)
Jenni Calder, *Chronicles of Conscience: A Study of George Orwell and Arthur Koestler* (Secker and Warburg, 1968)
Cyril Connolly, *Enemies of Promise* (Routledge and Kegan Paul, 1938)
Bernard Crick, *George Orwell: A Life* (Boston, Massachusetts: Little, Brown, 1980)
T. R. Fyvel, *George Orwell: A Personal Memoir* (New York: Macmillan, 1982)
George Orwell: A Collection of Critical Essays, ed. Raymond Williams (Englewood Cliffs, New Jersey: Prentice-Hall, 1974)
George Orwell and 'Nineteen Eighty-Four', ed. John Broderick (Washington, DC: Library of Congress, 1985)
George Orwell: The Critical Heritage, ed. Jeffrey Meyers (Routledge and Kegan Paul, 1975)
Wyndham Lewis, 'Orwell, or Two and Two Make Four', *The Writer and the Absolute* (Methuen, 1952)

Mary McCarthy, 'The Writing on the Wall', *New York Review of Books*, 30 January 1969, pp. 3–6.

Jeffrey Meyers, *A Reader's Guide to George Orwell* (Thames and Hudson, 1975)

Jeffrey Meyers and Valerie Meyers, *George Orwell: An Annotated Bibliography of Criticism* (New York: Garland, 1977)

Orwell Remembered, ed. Audrey Coppard and Bernard Crick (BBC, Ariel Books, 1984)

Patrick Reilly, *George Orwell: The Age's Adversary* (Macmillan, 1986)

John Rodden, *The Politics of Literary Reputation: The Making and Claiming of 'St George' Orwell* (Oxford: Oxford University Press, 1989)

Alan Sandison, *The Last Man in Europe: An Essay on George Orwell* (Macmillan, 1974)

Peter Stansky and William Abrahams, *The Unknown Orwell* (Constable, 1972)

Peter Stansky and William Abrahams, *Orwell: The Transformation* (Constable, 1979)

William Steinhoff, *George Orwell and the Origins of 'Nineteen Eighty-Four'* (Ann Arbor: University of Michigan Press, 1975)

Lionel Trilling, 'George Orwell and the Politics of Truth', *The Opposing Self* (New York: Viking, 1955)

Anthony West, 'George Orwell', *Principles and Persuasions* (New York: Harcourt, Brace, 1957)

Raymond Williams, *George Orwell* (New York: Viking, 1971)

George Woodcock, *The Crystal Spirit: A Study of George Orwell* (Boston, Massachusetts: Little, Brown, 1966); revised Edition (Fourth Estate, 1984)

The World of George Orwell, ed. Miriam Gross (Weidenfeld and Nicolson, 1971)

Alex Zwerdling, *Orwell and the Left* (New Haven, Connecticut: Yale University Press, 1974)

Index

154